RECIPES AND
PROJECTS FOR LITTLE HANDS

- AT THE -

FARMERS'
MARKET
WITH KIDS

BY LESLIE JONATH & ETHEL BRENNAN

PHOTOGRAPHS BY SHERI GIBLIN

CHRONICLE BOOKS

SAN FRANCISCO

We would like to thank all of the wonderful, curious, enthusiastic kids who helped us test, taste, and photograph recipes and Farmers' Market fun; Ethel's sons, Oscar and Raphael Rigobert, Leslie's nieces, Sarah and Monique Jonath, Sheri's lovely daughter Lucinda Muise and her niece Delilah Giblin, Josephine Thorton, Jonathan Hughes, Amélie and Clarisse Ritter, Jules and Adèle Salters, Matys and Morgan McMillin, Scarlet Dedini, Ignacio Hadjaj, and all the children we met at the Temescal Farmers' Market in Oakland. Thank you to the many farmers and vendors, also of the Temescal Farmers' Market, who let us photograph their beautiful, seasonal produce! We would also like to thank our friend Howard Garrison for donating pounds and pounds of peaches, plums, and nectarines for photographing!!! Thank you to Sheri Giblin, our beautiful and talented photographer, her amazing assistants, Shay Harrington and Kassandra Medeiros. Thank you to the great team at Chronicle Books including editors Bill LeBlond and Amy Treadwell, copy editor Judith Dunham, production coordinator Tera Killip, managing editor Doug Ogan, art director Alice Chau, the amazing food marketing and publicity team of Peter Perez and David Hawk, and our fabulous designer and friend Gretchen Scoble. Special thanks to friend and fellow stylist Alessandra Mortola for sharing her collection of props with us.

Library of Congress Cataloging-in-Publication Data available.
ISBN 978-0-8118-7502-8

Manufactured in China

Designed by Gretchen Scoble
Food and Prop styling by Ethel Brennan

10 9 8 7 6 5 4 3 2 1

Chronicle Books LLC
680 Second Street
San Francisco, California 94107
www.chroniclebooks.com

For my favorite farmers' market cooks, Sarah and Monique. —Leslie

*This book is dedicated to my lovely, inspirational mother, Georgeanne,
and my stepfather, Jim. Thank you for all your support and enthusiasm
for my various projects over the years! —Ethel*

Contents

Introduction

Every Sunday, we head to our local farmers' markets. Leslie meets her nieces, Monique and Sarah, at the Temescal Market in Oakland, while Ethel brings her twins, Oscar and Raphael, to the Alemany Market in San Francisco. The best thing about visiting a farmers' market is that you get to sample what's being sold—and we sample everything. The twins amble about, stuffing their mouths with strawberries and blueberries. Monique and Sarah like to sample cherry tomatoes. We enjoy seeing other families and talking to farmers as we load our bags with seasonal produce.

Even though our farmers' markets are in the midst of urban activity, going to the market makes us feel as if the farm has come to us. We pick up new facts about what we buy and new ideas for using what we tote home. José, who sells beautiful pears, might offer a wedge from a new Asian cultivar. Will, the strawberry vendor, is eager to point out that strawberries have their seeds on the outside. We might learn a tip for baking plums or discover a new type of pumpkin for carving. For the kids, going to the market is akin to going to a big party attended by lots of people having a good time. There is something different to taste and to do on every visit. Around the country, farmers' markets like ours have sprouted up in cities and towns, giving urbanites the opportunity to experience the bounty of the seasons.

The kids love the market, and cooking from our market purchases is one of our favorite ways to spend time with them. Throughout the year, we make recipes that highlight the versatility and seasonality of produce. Shopping and preparing something that celebrates food and the seasons have become weekly rituals we all look forward to.

If you've picked up this book, chances are you already shop at a farmers' market and are looking for new ways to enjoy the experience with your kids. Cooking after our market visits has inspired us to create dozens of food and craft recipes that double as family projects.

True to the spirit of a farmers' market, this book is organized by the seasons. For each season, we offer profiles of our favorite farmers' market fruits and vegetables, with handy tips on how to choose and store them, along with a list of varieties we particularly like. Most important, we share recipes that celebrate the time of year: dipping beet-dyed Easter eggs in spring, making berry jam in summer, drying grapes in fall, fermenting sauerkraut in winter. Many projects, such as dried-fruit bracelets, creamy apple butter, and berry-dyed T-shirts, make terrific seasonal gifts. Recipes such as tomato ketchup and cucumber pickles teach kids that foods they thought only came in bottles from the store can be prepared at home.

In choosing the recipes, we thought carefully about what made a recipe successful for kids and came up with the following criteria:

1. The recipes feature produce as the main ingredient and/or give kids tactile experience with the ingredient. Watermelon must be juiced for watermelon gelatin, for example, and red beets star in magenta beet cupcakes.

2. The recipes are fun for kids to make. Rolling dough, shelling beans, and mixing ingredients are easy and enjoyable tasks.

3. The recipes celebrate the seasons and seasonal holidays: making nectarine frozen yogurt in summer, mashing sweet potatoes with candied pecans for a Thanksgiving feast, sugaring lemon peel for holiday sweets.

4. The recipes often double as crafts and gifts for kids to give to family and friends. Jams, candies, and other preserves are as exciting to give as they are to make.

5. The recipes must be delicious and fun to eat.

There are many reasons we like to shop with kids at the farmers' market. Not only is the activity fun, but kids have the opportunity to meet the growers and learn about where food comes from. Once kids learn this, they will connect growing to cooking and ultimately to eating. Giving kids the power to make choices about what to buy and how to cook is a great way to encourage them to try new foods and to develop lifelong healthful eating habits. Tasting the varieties and learning their names might make even the pickiest young eaters change their minds about something they disliked in the past—or at least keep them entertained until the shopping is done.

Our hope is that this book will help you show your kids how to buy fresh, seasonal foods at the market and how to use them at home. We also hope that going to and cooking from the farmers' market will become a ritual in your lives just as it has in ours.

Cooking with Kids

This book was written with a child's sensibility and wonderment in mind. We chose the recipes based on our experience of what kids like to eat and which kitchen tasks they most enjoy.

Kids' skills vary wildly according to their age and other factors, so we include a broad range of recipes. Some are ideal for little hands new to the kitchen; others are for bigger, more experienced cooks. We tuck in quick, simple recipes for parents and kids on the go, as well as dishes with many steps for kids who like to spend time in the kitchen.

What your kids can do depends on their skill level and how comfortable you are putting tools and equipment, such as knives or a blender, in their hands. For example, young children can usually crack eggs, measure ingredients, grease pans, and rinse fruits and vegetables. Older kids can take on advanced tasks, such as chopping an onion, peeling an apple, or whipping egg whites. Each recipe lists what kids can generally do, but the final decision is yours because you know your kids best.

Ten Tips for Cooking with Kids

1. Before you go to the market, talk with your kids about what they want to make, then work together to jot down a list of the vegetables and fruits you need. When you're at the market, ask them to be on the lookout for the items on the list. If a child doesn't like an ingredient in the recipe, discuss what might make a good substitution. Don't like walnuts? Try pecans. Don't like peaches? Substitute plums. Here is the chance to think about how to make the recipe a good fit for the whole family.

2. Talk to your kids about safety and cleanliness. Let them know that they need to be careful around sharp knives, hot pans, and electrical appliances. Stress the importance of always washing hands with warm water and soap before they touch food; rinsing fruits and vegetables well before using them; and cleaning up spills, work surfaces, and tools as they go along. We like to wear aprons to keep our clothes clean and to make it official that we are cooking.

3. Read through the recipe together. If one of your kids is old enough, have him or her read it out loud. Go through all the ingredients to make sure you have everything, pulling them out of the cupboards and refrigerator as you go. This is a good process for any cook and is a good habit to start young. (How many times have you stopped halfway through a recipe because you don't have eggs, for instance, or the right pan?) An older child can set up the ingredients in the order they are used in the recipe.

4. Set up a good workspace. Make sure that it is not too high and that it is big enough so everyone can work comfortably. A kitchen table is often ideal. Or you may need to put a chair or two—they should be sturdy and the seats perfectly flat—next to a counter for little ones to stand on.

5. Prepare the ingredients ahead of time. Chop, slice, or shave ingredients before you start making the recipe. Determine who should do each task. Your kids can help measure liquids and dry ingredients like flour. Or, for example, they can shell beans while you chop onions.

6. Know what your kids can do alone or with minimal help. Generally, older kids can chop, stir ingredients as they cook in a pan, and put pans in the oven. Younger kids like to measure sugar and flour, crack eggs, stir batter, shell beans, and pick through berries to look for rotten fruit. Check the "Kids Can" section in each recipe for the tasks that most kids can perform. You can give even the youngest child an ingredient and a safe tool—a small bowl of flour and a measuring spoon, a banana and a plastic knife—to play with while you do the work.

7. Know what you don't want your kids to do. Using sharp knives, pulling hot pans out of the oven, cutting corn kernels off the cob, running the food processor—these are the kinds of tasks that you may want to handle yourself. A little helper can hold a mixer or push the button on a food processor by putting his or her hand over yours. Take your time ceding tasks to your kids until you feel confident of their skill level.

8. Be sure to have something for kids to nibble on. Baking an apple pie? Slice up an extra apple. Mixing a batch of blackberry jam? Buy an extra basket for snacking.

9. Praise often, be patient, and don't let messes upset you. If a mistake is made, don't worry. A cake batter whipped up with salt instead of sugar can be turned into an amusing family story.

10. Enjoy, enjoy, enjoy!

SPRING

Spring marks the time of awakening when the quiet calm of the winter market is invaded by bright lettuces, aromatic herbs, and early stone fruit. It's easier to convince the kids to get up and out to gather floral-scented apricots, juicy cherries, and bunches of brightly colored carrots. Spring is a time of appreciation, when we enjoy the year's first tender vegetables and fresh fruit pies and the warmth of delicate sunshine.

Apricots

Apricot means "precious" in Latin, an adjective that describes how people feel about the luscious fruits when they first arrive in the market. Apricots have a delicate floral flavor and aroma, so it is not surprising that they are in the same family as roses. Most commercially sold apricots are picked early and lack flavor, but you can find many delicious varieties at farmers' markets. Perfectly ripe apricots are wonderful in baked goods and pies as well as in savory dishes.

Choosing: Apricots should be fragrant and slightly soft. Ripe apricots have a very short shelf life, so it's best to buy them the day that you are going to use them. Avoid bruised apricots, although slightly over-ripe specimens are fine for making jam (see recipe for berry jam, page 56).

Storing: Use ripe apricots the day that you buy them. If you end up with some that are not quite ready, place them in a paper bag and seal the top to encourage ripening. Do not store in the refrigerator.

Varieties: Blenheim, Golden Sweet, Harcot, Moorpark, Orange Red, Robada

Upside-Down Apricot Skillet Cake

If your kids like to hang upside down on the monkey bars, they will appreciate this upside-down cake. We use apricots, but many other fruits, such as peaches, plums, and nectarines, can be substituted. Skillet cakes are fun for kids to make because they are simple and foolproof. Serve topped with scoops of vanilla ice cream. [SERVES 6 TO 8]

6 tablespoons unsalted butter

1 cup sugar

2 pounds soft, ripe apricots, halved and pitted

1 cup all-purpose flour

1 teaspoon baking powder

¼ teaspoon salt

4 eggs

KIDS CAN
halve and pit the apricots • place apricot halves facedown in the pan • measure and mix ingredients • help pour the batter over the apricots

1. Preheat the oven to 350°F.

2. Place an ovenproof skillet over medium heat and melt 5 table-spoons of the butter. As the butter melts, lift and turn the pan to coat the sides. Sprinkle ¼ cup of the sugar evenly over the bottom of the pan. Place the apricots, skin-side down, in the pan, arranging them in concentric circles. Remove the pan from the heat.

3. In a bowl, whisk together the flour, baking powder, and salt.

4. Separate the eggs, putting the whites into a large bowl and the yolks into a smaller one. In a small pan over medium heat, melt the remaining 1 tablespoon butter. Whisk it into the egg yolks. With a handheld mixer set on medium speed or with a clean whisk, beat the egg whites just until they form firm peaks. Do not overbeat. Fold the remaining ¾ cup sugar into the egg whites, about ¼ cup at a time. Then very slowly fold in the egg yolk mixture, about one-fourth at a time. Finally, fold in the flour mixture, about ¼ cup at a time. Pour the batter over the apricots and spread to cover them evenly.

5. Bake until a toothpick inserted into the center of the cake comes out clean, 30 to 40 minutes. Let the cake stand in the pan for at least 10 minutes. Run a knife around the inside of the pan. Invert a large plate over the pan. Firmly holding both the plate and the pan, turn them over. Lift off the pan. Serve the cake warm or at room temperature, cut into wedges.

Asparagus

Asparagus spears are the shoots or sprouts that appear before the plant matures.

The spears can be as thin as a pencil to nearly an inch in diameter. Thin spears can be easier for little mouths to chew but are flimsier for dipping. You and your kids can decide which thickness you prefer. At some markets, you might find white asparagus or purple asparagus. A blanching process is used to create white asparagus. Earth is mounded over the new shoots so that they grow without being exposed to light. (In the right conditions, an asparagus spear can grow up to a foot in one day!) Purple asparagus is a separate variety with a slightly different—and some say sweeter—flavor.

Choosing: The stalks should be firm and even in color. The tips should be tightly packed, and the stem ends should not be dry or woody.

Storing: It is best to eat asparagus within 3 days of purchase. To store the spears, wrap them in a plastic bag and place in a vegetable bin in the refrigerator.

Varieties: Mary Washington, Purple Passion

Asparagus Spears with Yogurt-Herb Dip

Asparagus is the perfect finger food for kids. Even little kids (as young as two) can get the hang of dipping the spears. Experimenting with different flavors of dips will encourage children to test their culinary palates in the kitchen. If your kids don't like fresh herbs, you can substitute other flavors, such as fresh lemon juice and grated zest. [SERVES 4]

1 tray of ice cubes

1 pound asparagus

½ cup low-fat plain yogurt

1 teaspoon finely chopped chives

1 teaspoon finely chopped flat-leaf parsley

¼ teaspoon salt

1. Bring a large pot of water to a boil. While the water is heating, fill a bowl with water and add the ice cubes.

2. Hold each asparagus spear at both ends. Gently bend the stem end until it breaks—it will snap at a natural point. Slip the spears into the boiling water and cook until the color is vibrant, 3 to 4 minutes. Drain the spears and put them in the ice water. Let them sit in the ice water until chilled, about 10 minutes. Remove the spears from the water and pat dry.

3. In a small bowl, combine the yogurt, chives, parsley, and salt. Mix well with a fork.

4. Arrange the asparagus on a platter. Place the bowl of dip at one end of the platter and serve.

KIDS CAN
unmold the ice cubes • snap the asparagus spears • pull the spears out of the ice water • measure and mix the ingredients for the dip

Beets, Radishes, Carrots, and Turnips

Root vegetables are available year-round but are especially tender and flavorful in spring. Carrots range from walnut-size round specimens to foot-long tapers in hues of orange, purple, yellow, red, or white. Beets also come in many colors: shades of red and yellow and even striped. You may also see round or oval radishes in pastel pink, purple, or white. Asian radishes include the long white daikon and round green radishes with scarlet flesh such as the watermelon radish. All radishes are peppery but vary in their degree of spiciness.

Choosing: Beets, carrots, radishes, and turnips should be firm to the touch, and the root ends shouldn't have too many tiny roots. Select smooth root vegetables that are free of blemishes or cracks. Avoid those that are green at the stem end. The attached leaves should be green.

Storage: Remove the tops from all roots, but don't toss out those from beets and turnips! Wash and dry them and store in plastic bags for up to 3 days. Beet and turnip greens can be sautéed or added to soups and stews. Store beets, carrots, turnips, and radishes in plastic bags in the refrigerator. Beets, turnips, and carrots will keep for up to 3 weeks, radishes for 1 week.

Varieties: beets: Bull's Blood, Chioggia, Detroit Dark Red, Yellow Detroit; carrots: King Midas, Lunar White, Purple Haze, Round Romeo, Samurai, Yellowstone; radishes: Cherry Belle, daikon, Easter Egg, French Breakfast, Icicle, watermelon; turnips: American Purple Top, Just Right

Chocolate-Beet Cupcakes

If there is one way to get kids to eat beets, it will be in these rich chocolate cupcakes. Inspired by red velvet cake, the batter is a glorious magenta color. Adding chocolate turns the batter purple before it is baked into delicious cupcakes that don't taste at all like beets. You'll need to let the beets cool before grating them, so allow an hour or two to make this recipe. Grating the beets can also be very messy, which is fun for kids. Parents be forewarned—you might want to keep a bowl of soapy water nearby for quick cleanups.

[MAKES ABOUT 12 CUPCAKES]

3 to 4 small red beets

2 ounces bittersweet chocolate

1 cup flour

1 teaspoon baking soda

½ teaspoon salt

½ cup unsalted butter, at room temperature

1 cup sugar

2 eggs

1 teaspoon pure vanilla extract

Powdered sugar for dusting

1. Place the beets in a saucepan, add water to cover, and bring to a boil over high heat. Reduce heat to a simmer and cook the beets until tender, about 35 minutes. Drain in a colander and let cool.

2. When beets are cool enough to handle, grate them on the large holes of a box grater. You should have a total of 1 cup grated beets.

3. In a heatproof bowl, melt the chocolate in a microwave, heating it in increments of 30 seconds at a time, for a total of 1½ minutes. Or you can place the bowl over (but not touching) simmering water in a small saucepan. Stir the melted chocolate until it is smooth, then let it cool slightly.

4. Preheat the oven to 350°F. Line 12 standard muffin cups with paper liners.

continued

5. In a small bowl, combine the flour, baking soda, and salt. In a large bowl, beat the butter and sugar with a handheld mixer until light and fluffy. Beat in the eggs and vanilla. Add the grated beets and beat until the mixture is smooth and evenly bright magenta. Beat in the melted chocolate. Gradually add the flour mixture and beat until fully combined. Spoon the batter into the lined muffin cups, filling each about two-thirds full.

6. Bake until the tops spring back when touched and a toothpick inserted into the center of a cupcake comes out clean, 20 to 25 minutes. Put the pan on a wire rack and let the cupcakes cool completely. Dust the tops with powdered sugar by placing sugar in a fine-mesh strainer, positioning over a cupcake, and tapping gently. Keep the cupcakes in an airtight container 3 to 5 days.

Roasted Root Salad

Roasting root vegetables brings out the natural sugars, giving them a faint sweet cara-melized flavor, a quality that is pleasing to kids. Look for baby or small vegetables, which can be used whole. When you're at the market, you and your kids can seek out beets and carrots in a variety of colors. Baby turnips are mild and sweet in flavor. Look for white ones or purple-top varieties. [SERVES 4]

6 baby carrots

6 baby beets

6 baby turnips

2 tablespoons olive oil

1 teaspoon salt

FOR THE DRESSING

2 teaspoons balsamic vinegar

¼ teaspoon coarse sea salt

2 tablespoons extra-virgin olive oil

1 cup salad greens, torn into pieces

1. Preheat the oven to 400°F.

2. If the tops are still attached to the carrots, beets, and turnips, twist and pull off. Use a knife to trim the ends.

3. Place the vegetables in a shallow roasting pan in a single layer. Drizzle the olive oil over the vegetables and toss to coat them. Sprinkle the salt over the vegetables and toss them again. Spread them in a single layer. Roast the vegetables, turning them several times, until they are tender when pierced with a fork, about 45 min-utes. Let the vegetables cool in the pan.

4. To make the dressing: Choose a small jar with a lid or an airtight plastic container. Combine the vinegar, salt, and olive oil in the jar or container. Shake it well to mix the dressing.

5. Put the roasted vegetables in a bowl. Add the salad greens. Pour the dressing over the vegetables and greens and toss to coat them with the dressing before serving.

KIDS CAN
rinse carrots, beets, and turnips and remove the tops • coat vegetables with oil • rinse, dry, and tear greens into pieces • measure and mix dressing ingredients

Radish Tea Party Sandwiches

Young kids love a tea party, and these sandwiches are worthy of Alice in Wonderland. You can use any radish variety from the market, including Easter Egg radishes, which come in shades of lavender and tea party pink. The recipe calls for butter, but cream cheese, spread generously on the bread, is a delectable alternative. Serve the sandwiches with chilled strawberry lemonade or iced tea. [SERVES 6]

2 bunches radishes

3 tablespoons salted butter

12 thin slices of rye bread
or other sandwich bread

1. If the radish tops are still attached, twist them and pull off. Cut the radishes into thin slices.

2. Lightly spread the butter on one side of each slice of bread. Arrange the slices buttered-side up. For each sandwich, arrange a layer of radish slices on a slice of buttered bread. Place another slice of bread, buttered-side down. Cut the sandwiches into quarters to serve.

KIDS CAN
remove the radish tops and rinse and slice the radishes • butter the bread • assemble the sandwiches

Easter Eggs Dyed with Beets and Onion Skins

Although dyes for Easter eggs are always available in stores, natural dyes are easy to make using beets and onions of different colors. White eggs turn brighter colors than brown eggs, which take on muted tones. The eggs can be cooked up to 3 days ahead and stored in their cartons in the refrigerator. Beet dyes work best when hot, so parent supervision is important. [MAKES 18 DYED EGGS]

FOR BEET-DYED EGGS

12 eggs

6 medium red beets

2 tablespoons white vinegar

Cheesecloth

6 medium yellow beets

1 tablespoon ground turmeric

KIDS CAN
grate the beets • dip the eggs in the dye • soak the onion skins and wrap around the eggs • unfurl the skins after eggs are cooked

1. To beet-dye the eggs: Place the eggs in a large pot. Add enough cold water to cover the eggs. Bring to a boil over high heat, then turn off the heat. Let the eggs stand in the hot water for 20 minutes. Remove the eggs from the water and pat them dry.

2. To dye the eggs red, trim the stems and root ends from the red beets. Grate the beets on a box grater. They do not need to be peeled. Place the grated beets in a pot and add 3 cups water. Bring to a boil over high heat, reduce the heat to medium, and cook for 30 minutes. Stir in the vinegar and strain through a colander lined with cheesecloth. Discard the grated beets. Pour the beet dye into a small glass or ceramic bowl; you should have about 1 cup. Gently add 2 eggs at a time to the dye and let stand for 10 to 15 minutes. The dye works best when hot, so reheat it as needed.

3. To dye the eggs yellow, trim the stem and root ends from the yellow beets. The skins of yellow beets have a greenish tint that can muddy the color, so unlike red beets they need to be peeled. Grate the peeled beets on a box grater. Place the grated beets in a pot and add 3 cups water and the turmeric. Follow the same method as for the red beets, reheating the dye as needed.

continued

FOR ONION SKIN–DYED EGGS

Skins of 12 to 14 onions, both red and yellow

6 pieces of fabric, preferably nylon pantyhose, each about 8 inches square

6 eggs

20 to 30 rubber bands

1. To onion skin–dye the eggs: Fill a large bowl with water and put the onion skins in the water. Let the skins soften in the water for about 10 minutes. One by one, put the fabric squares in the water. Squeeze out the squares until they are just moistened. Wrap 4 or 5 onion skins around each egg to cover it completely. Place the egg in the middle of a fabric square. Bring up the corners of the fabric and wrap the fabric snugly around the egg so that the onion skins press tightly against the egg. Wrap rubber bands around the fabric to hold it in place.

2. Put the wrapped eggs in a pot. Pour in enough cold water to cover the eggs. Bring to a boil over high heat. Boil the eggs for 6 to 7 minutes. Drain the water from the pot and run cold water into the pot to cool the eggs. Carefully remove the rubber bands and then the fabric from the eggs. Peel off the onion skins. The eggshells will have absorbed the swirling pattern of the onion skins. Let the eggs dry.

Cherries

Cherries are one of the first stone fruits to reach the market in spring. The two main types are the sweet cherry (also called wild cherry) and the sour cherry (also called tart cherry). Sour cherries are excellent in preserves and pies, though they are harder to find. Sweet cherries are wonderful eaten out of hand and cooked in pies and other desserts and in savory dishes. Cherries need to be pitted—a task that can be entertaining for kids. You can find a cherry pitter at grocery stores and cookware stores.

Choosing: All cherries should still have their stems attached and be clean and dry. A ripe cherry should be heavy for its size. Avoid cherries that are hard, small, light in color, or are soft or sticky.

Storing: Store cherries in a wide, shallow bowl in the refrigerator, covered with a paper towel or kitchen towel, for up to 4 days. Do not wash the cherries until you are ready to use them. To freeze cherries, rinse, drain, and dry them, remove the pits, then spread the cherries evenly on a baking sheet and freeze. Place the frozen cherries in a lock-top freezer bag. They will keep for up to 1 year.

Varieties: Bing, Brooks, Burlat, Chapman, Lambert, Lapin, Morello, Montmorency, Queen Anne, Rainier, Royal Anne, Ruby, Stella, Van

Cherry Turnovers

Your kids may be unable to resist eating these turnovers straight out of the oven. No time for making dough? You can substitute store-bought pie crust. Using a cherry pitter takes some dexterity. Once kids learn how to handle it, pitting the cherries is fun. Teach them to watch for the pit to pop out of the device, as some pits may get stuck. [MAKES 4 TURNOVERS]

Flaky Pastry Dough (page 79)

2 cups cherries, stemmed, pitted, and halved

Juice of ½ lemon

½ cup sugar

1 tablespoon cornstarch

2 tablespoons water

1 egg lightly beaten with 1 tablespoon water

KIDS CAN
rinse the cherries, remove the stems, and pit cherries • measure ingredients for, mix, and roll the dough • fill and fold the turnovers

1. Preheat the oven to 350°F. Line a baking sheet with parchment paper.

2. Prepare the dough as directed. Gather the dough into a ball and divide into four even balls. Pat each ball flat to create a disk about 1 inch thick. Wrap the disks in plastic wrap and refrigerate for at least 30 minutes. They can be refrigerated for up to 24 hours.

3. Put the cherries in a bowl. Add the lemon juice, sugar, and cornstarch. Add the water and stir gently to combine the ingredients.

4. On a lightly floured work surface, roll out each disk of chilled dough until it is about 6 inches in diameter and ¼ inch thick. Place the dough rounds on the baking sheet. Spoon about ½ cup of the filling onto half of each round, leaving about ½ inch uncovered around the edge. Using a pastry brush, paint the beaten egg around the entire edge of the round. Fold the uncovered side of the round over the filling. Using a fork, press the edges together. With the fork, gently prick the tops of each turnover three or four times. Paint the tops with a bit more of the beaten egg.

5. Bake the turnovers until they are golden brown and the filling is oozing slightly from the edges, 20 to 25 minutes. Serve immediately.

Herbs

Teaching kids how to use herbs helps widen their understanding of seasoning food. Herbs add flavor, texture, and aroma to savory and sweet preparations. Stirring them into sauces or marinades or sprinkling them over finished recipes is a simple way to experiment. Herbs can be categorized in two ways: green or woody. Green herbs, such as chives, parsley, dill, and cilantro, are delicate and need to be used shortly after purchase. Woody herbs, such as rosemary, thyme, oregano, lemon verbena, and lavender, are much sturdier, dry well, and keep fresh longer. You can encourage your kids to add herbs to simple everyday dishes including scrambled eggs and garden salads.

Choosing: For both woody and green herbs, the stems should be freshly cut, not browned, and the tops lively and perky, not wilted.

Storing: Treat both types as cut flowers and keep them in a glass of water on the kitchen counter or in the refrigerator. Or wrap the herbs in paper towels and store in plastic bags in the refrigerator. Use herbs within 1 week. Woody herbs will dry nicely when left on a countertop in a bowl.

Varieties: chervil, chives, cilantro, dill, garlic chives, lavender, lemon verbena, oregano, parsley (flat leaf and curly leaf), purple basil, rosemary, sage, thai basil, thyme

Mix-and-Match Pesto

Derived from the Italian word *pestare*, which means "to pound or crush," *pesto* refers to a sauce made from fresh basil leaves, pine nuts, and pecorino or Parmesan cheese. Many kids love pesto served on spaghetti and other pasta shapes. It is also delicious on omelets or as a topping for grilled meat and fish. The recipe here calls for basil, but you could substitute parsley or cilantro. Instead of pine nuts, you can try walnuts or almonds, or omit the nuts. Mixing the pesto with a food processor is quick and easy, but if you have a mortar and pestle, your kids will have fun mashing and stirring the ingredients.

[MAKES ABOUT 1 CUP (ENOUGH FOR 1 POUND PASTA)]

1 clove garlic

¼ teaspoon salt

2 tablespoons pine nuts, toasted

2 cups packed basil leaves

¼ cup grated pecorino or Parmesan cheese

1 tablespoon freshly squeezed lemon juice

½ cup extra-virgin olive oil

1. Place the garlic, salt, nuts, basil, cheese, lemon juice, and oil in a food processor. Pulse until smooth.

2. If you are making the pesto with a mortar and pestle, put the garlic and salt in the mortar. Use the pestle to pound and stir the garlic and salt until they form a paste. Then add the nuts and basil and continue to pound and stir until the basil leaves and nuts are reduced to a paste and all the ingredients are well combined. Add the cheese and lemon juice and again pound and stir. When all the ingredients are mixed to a paste, slowly pour in the oil, stirring constantly with the pestle. You can pour the oil as your child stirs, or your child can pour while you stir.

3. Using a spatula, scrape the pesto into an airtight container. It will keep in the refrigerator for up to 1 week. You can also freeze the pesto in small portions (a freezer tray works well for this) to use throughout the year.

KIDS CAN
remove the herb leaves from the stems and rinse • grate the cheese • measure the ingredients • help mix the pesto

Herb Bouquets

The best part of creating herb bouquets is that they smell good while you are assembling them. Fresh herb bouquets can be used as centerpieces. You can later hang them upside down to dry. Fresh or dried, the bouquets make excellent gifts. Dried herbs taste very different from fresh herbs because, as the herbs dry, the essential oils and flavors intensify, making dried herbs a good choice for slow-cooked recipes, such as sauce or stews. Both fresh and dried herbs can be used to brew herbal teas and infusions. [MAKES 8 BOUQUETS]

3 bunches rosemary

3 bunches sage

3 bunches lemon verbena

1 bunch lavender

Eight 12-inch lengths of
  kitchen string or ribbon

1. Spread out the herb branches on a work surface. Arrange the herbs to create eight bouquets of the same size, mixing the different types of herbs. Trim the stems so they are even and then tie each bouquet tightly with string or ribbon. To keep the bouquets fresh, place them in jars or vases filled with water.

2. To dry the bouquets, hang them upside down. They will dry in about 1 week. When the herbs are dry, you can remove the leaves from the stems and store them in an airtight container for up to 6 months.

KIDS CAN
cut the string or
ribbon • arrange the
herb branches • tie off
the bouquets

Lettuces

At farmers' markets, you will see lettuces in many shapes, sizes, and colors. Some come as tightly wrapped heads like iceberg, and others are looser heads like butter lettuce and romaine, a long torpedo shape prized for its tender green heart. Other varieties, such as red and green oak leaf, are called "loose leaf" lettuces because the leaves can be easily plucked from the head.

Choosing: All types of lettuce should be free of bruised or brownish leaves. Tightly packed heads such as romaine should have a firm inner heart surrounded by unblemished, bright green outer leaves.

Storing: Tightly packed heads of lettuce will keep in the refrigerator, in a plastic bag, for 5 to 7 days. Loose-leaf types can be stored in a plastic bag for up to 3 days. It is best not to rinse lettuces before storing, as the added moisture promotes decay, shortening the storage time.

Varieties: Bibb, butter, iceberg, little gem, red and green oak leaf, romaine

Vietnamese-Style Lettuce Wraps

Light, refreshing, and easy to prepare, lettuce wraps are an ideal do-it-with-kids dish. Not only do kids help ready the filling ingredients, but each person at the table puts together his or her own wrap. For this reason, the wraps are a fun party dish. This recipe is best with a big loose-leaf lettuce such as butter or Bibb because the shape of the leaf makes it easy to wrap around the filling. But if you like, you can substitute other varieties such as romaine. Almonds or cashews may be used in place of the peanuts. Rice stick noodles and fish sauce can be found in the Asian section of many grocery stores. [SERVES 6 TO 8]

½ pound thin rice stick noodles

1 medium carrot, grated

2 tablespoons peanut oil

¼ cup chopped cilantro

¼ cup chopped basil

¼ cup finely chopped green onion tops

¼ cup chopped mint

¼ cup chopped dry-roasted peanuts

1. Prepare the noodles according to the package directions. When the noodles are cool enough to handle, cut them roughly into 4-inch lengths. This makes them easier to handle. Place the noodles in a medium bowl.

2. In a large bowl, toss together the carrot, peanut oil, cilantro, basil, green onion tops, and mint. Put the peanuts in a small bowl.

continued

KIDS CAN
cut the noodles • grate the carrot • rinse and dry the lettuce leaves • pull herb leaves from the stems, then rinse and dry them • measure the ingredients for the wraps and sauce

FOR THE DIPPING SAUCE

¼ cup sugar

½ cup warm water

¼ cup fish sauce

¼ cup rice vinegar

2 tablespoons freshly squeezed
  lime juice

2 cloves garlic, minced

1 Thai chile, seeded and minced
  (optional)

8 to 10 large lettuce leaves

3. To make the dipping sauce: Put the sugar and warm water in a small bowl, then whisk until the sugar is dissolved. Add the fish sauce, vinegar, lime juice, garlic, and chile (if using) and whisk again. Pour the sauce into individual small bowls.

4. Put the lettuce leaves on a plate and bring to the table with the bowls containing the noodles, the carrot mixture, and the peanuts. Arrange the bowls of sauce on the table.

5. Everyone assembles his or her own wraps. Place a lettuce leaf on a plate. Line the center with noodles. Spoon the carrot mixture over the noodles and then sprinkle with peanuts. Pick up one side of the leaf, place over the filling, and roll the leaf into a cylinder. Dip in the sauce.

Strawberries

According to one story, strawberries got their name from the layer of straw that farmers spread around the plants to protect them from frost. The perfect size for little hands, strawberries are a favorite fruit for kids to eat out of hand. Kids also like them sliced and topped with whipped cream or yogurt. Unlike other fruits, strawberries have their seeds on the outside, visible as tiny yellow dots. On average, there are 200 seeds on every berry.

Choosing: Select berries that are bright red and shiny with dark green stem caps and leaves. Avoid berries with green or white patches. Since strawberries do not ripen after being picked, sample the berries to make sure they are sweet and ripe.

Storing: Strawberries lose flavor and moisture as soon as they are picked, so it is best to eat them the day of purchase. If you need to store the berries, layer them in a large container, separating the layers with paper towels. Do not rinse the berries before storing them. Cover and refrigerate for 3 to 5 days. To freeze the berries, cut the hulls and stems from the berries, leave the berries whole or cut them in half, arrange in a single layer on a baking sheet, and freeze. Place the frozen berries in a lock-top freezer bag. They will keep for up to 1 year.

Varieties: Chandler, Early Glow, Firecracker, Fraises des Bois, Seascape, Sparkle

Create Jar Labels

Making labels is the perfect way for kids to personalize a project such as making jam, jelly, or other preserves. Have ready premade sticker labels or hang tags, one per jar. For each hang tag, you will need an 8-inch length of ⅛-inch-wide ribbon or kitchen twine. Kids can use colored pens or pencils for writing the name of the recipe and the date and for decorating the labels and tags. After the jars are filled and sealed, stick on the labels or tie on the tags.

Strawberry Freezer Jam

A simple mixture of crushed strawberries, pectin, and sugar magically comes together to make a sweet, colorful jam. The recipe involves no cooking, so kids can nearly do it all (except for sterilizing the jars)! After the jam is removed from the freezer, it will keep for up to a month in the refrigerator. This recipe calls for Sure-Jell, but you can use other brands. [MAKES 6 HALF-PINT JARS]

3 pounds strawberries

½ cup sugar

One 1¾-ounce package
 dry pectin such as Sure-Jell

KIDS CAN
rinse the berries •
remove the stems from
the berries • crush the
berries • mix the jam and
spoon it into the jars

1. Thoroughly wash six half-pint freezer-safe canning jars and their lids and screw bands. Put the jars, lids, and screw bands in a large pot and add water to cover. Bring to a boil and continue to boil for 15 minutes to sterilize the jars, lids, and bands. Using tongs, lift the jars, lids, and bands from the hot water and dry thoroughly.

2. Pick through the berries, discarding any rotten ones. Remove the stem ends and hulls. Coarsely chop the strawberries and place them in a large bowl. Using the back of a wooden spoon (or your hands), crush the berries to make a pulp. In another bowl, stir together the sugar and pectin. Stir the pectin mixture into the berry pulp and mix together with a wooden spoon for 3 to 5 minutes until it begins to thicken.

3. Ladle the jam into the sterilized jars, leaving a ½-inch headspace. Wipe each jar rim clean with a damp towel, then top with a lid and seal tightly with a screw band. Let the jars stand for 30 minutes. Label the jars with the recipe name and date and put in the freezer. The jam can be frozen for up to 1 year.

Strawberry Corn Muffins

Moist and a little bit crumbly, these strawberry-studded muffins are inspired by a similar version served at the Westside Bakery Café in Berkeley, California. In summer, the muffins can be made with blackberries, blueberries, or apricots or peaches cut into ½-inch cubes. You can also add chopped nuts, such as pecans or walnuts, along with the fruit to contribute a little extra crunch. [MAKES 12 MUFFINS]

1 cup strawberries, stemmed, hulled, and sliced

1 cup cornmeal

1 cup all-purpose flour

½ cup sugar, plus 1 tablespoon for topping

1 tablespoon baking powder

½ teaspoon salt

2 eggs

1¼ cups buttermilk

2 tablespoons unsalted butter, melted

1. Preheat the oven to 350°F. Line 12 standard muffin cups with paper liners.

2. Pick through the berries, discarding any rotten ones. Remove the stem ends and hulls. Slice the berries.

3. In a medium bowl, combine the cornmeal, flour, ½ cup sugar, the baking powder, and salt. Stir to mix. In a large bowl, whisk together the eggs and buttermilk. Using a rubber spatula, gently fold in the flour mixture, one-third at time, being careful not to overmix the batter. Gently fold in the melted butter and sliced strawberries.

4. Fill the muffin cups to within ½ inch of the rims. Then sprinkle the remaining sugar evenly over the tops.

5. Bake until a toothpick inserted into the center of a muffin comes out clean, 20 to 25 minutes. Let the muffins cool in the pan for 10 minutes. Remove the muffins from the pan and put them on a wire rack to finish cooling. Keep the muffins in an airtight container for 3 days or in the refrigerator for 1 week.

KIDS CAN
rinse stem, hull, and slice the strawberries • place liners in the muffin cups • measure the ingredients and mix the batter • spoon the batter into the muffin cups

Peas and Fava Beans

You may find different types of peas at the market. English peas, also called shelling peas, are enclosed in a tough pod. Sugar snap peas have a edible tender pod and can be used when the peas are still immature. Even when the peas are fully developed, the pod remains tender, and the peas can be shelled or left in the pod. Snow peas have an edible, tender, flat pod and are eaten when the peas are undeveloped. Fava beans have a very thick, bright-green pod lined with soft, spongy padding. Each sweet, nutty-flavored bean inside is covered with a thin but tough skin that can be bitter but is easy to remove.

Choosing: Pods should be firm and crisp, not wilted, and free of blemishes. Fava pods can have slight scars and blemishes, as their thickness protects the beans inside.

Storing: Keep beans and peas in plastic bags in the refrigerator for 5 to 7 days. Over longer storage, the starches in peas and beans will continue to develop, and the sweet flavor and tender texture will fade.

Varieties: common fava beans; shelling peas: Blue Pod, Pioneer; snow peas: Golden Sweet, Oregon Giant; sugar snap peas: Sweet Ann, Super Sugar Snap

Fava Bean Purée with Crunchy Croutons

After fava beans are shelled, their thick skins still need to be peeled—a fun task for kids. Cooking the beans briefly in boiling water makes the beans very easy to slip from the skins. Here, the peeled beans are blended into a thick, creamy purée for spreading on toasted bread. [MAKES ABOUT 25 CROUTONS]

1 tray of ice cubes

3 pounds fava beans, shelled

¼ cup extra-virgin olive oil

½ teaspoon coarse sea salt

2 tablespoons freshly squeezed
  lemon juice

FOR THE CROUTONS

2 cloves garlic, crushed

1 sourdough baguette, cut into
  slices about ½ inch thick (about
  25 slices)

2 tablespoons extra-virgin olive oil

1 tablespoon crumbled feta cheese
  for garnish

1. Bring a medium saucepan of water to a boil. While the water is heating, fill a bowl with water and add the ice cubes. Add the beans to the boiling water and cook for 1 minute. Drain the beans and put them in the ice water. Let them sit in the ice water until chilled, about 5 minutes. Drain the beans.

2. Pinch off one end of the skin covering each bean and slip out the bean. Put the beans, olive oil, salt, and lemon juice in a food processor. Process until smooth.

3. To make the croutons: Preheat the oven to 350°F. Rub the garlic on both sides of each bread slice. Put the slices in a bowl. Drizzle the olive oil over the slices and toss. Arrange the slices on a baking sheet. Toast in the oven, turning the slices several times, until they are golden brown, 15 to 20 minutes.

4. When the croutons are cool enough to handle, slather on the fava bean purée. Sprinkle each with a pinch of the crumbled feta cheese before serving.

KIDS CAN
unmold the ice cubes • shell the beans • remove the beans from their skins • rub the bread slices with garlic • spread the purée on the croutons

Pasta with Peas and Browned Butter

Fresh shelling peas at the peak of ripeness are tender and sweet and barely need to be cooked. Tossing blanched peas with nutty-flavored browned butter, chive blossoms, and pasta is a simple, tasty dish perfect for a quick lunch or dinner. Another edible flower from the market could be used as a pretty garnish. You can substitute sugar snap peas or fava beans (for instructions on peeling, see page 47) for the shelling peas. [SERVES 4]

1 tray of ice cubes

1 pound shelling peas, shelled

1 pound dried fettuccine

2 tablespoons unsalted butter

¼ teaspoon salt

1 tablespoon chive blossoms (optional)

KIDS CAN
unmold the ice cubes • shell the peas • help drain the cooled peas • mix the pasta and peas • garnish the finished dish

1. Bring a medium saucepan half filled with water to a boil. While the water is heating, fill a bowl with water and add the ice cubes. Add the peas to the boiling water and cook for 1 minute. Drain the peas and put them in the ice water to chill for 3 to 5 minutes. Drain.

2. Bring a large pot of water to a boil and cook the pasta according to the directions on the package. Drain the pasta.

3. In a skillet over medium heat, melt the butter. Continue to cook it, stirring often, until the butter just begins to brown. Add the peas and stir to coat them with the butter. Add the pasta and toss to coat with the butter.

4. Put the pasta and peas in a bowl. Sprinkle with the salt and the chive blossoms, if using. Serve immediately.

SUMMER

The stands at farmers' markets are piled high with green beans, zucchini, corn, nectarines, peaches, berries, plums, and melons. Hand-drawn signs often herald unusual or short-season varieties, such as Arctic Supreme peaches, Elephant Heart plums, and yellow wax beans. Tomatoes in a rainbow of colors are on display: red, green, orange, and purple. This is the best time of year for you and your kids to make roasted-tomato sauce, bake fruit cobblers, freeze watermelon ice pops, and churn blackberry ice cream. You can put up refrigerator pickles and berry jam so that you can enjoy the summer bounty long after the season has ended.

Beans

At summer markets, you'll find yellow and purple wax beans and different varieties of green beans (also called snap or string beans), including slender haricots verts. Fresh pod beans like these can be eaten pod and all. Shelling beans, the other general category, are sold once the beans have matured and can be slipped from the pod. They can also be harvested early and used in the same fashion as green beans. Most shelling beans are sold fresh at the farmers' markets during the peak of the season, before being dried. Removing beans from their pods is a great way to spend time with your kids—and get help in the kitchen!

Choosing: Green and wax beans should be smooth and firm. The pod of a shell bean should be a little bumpy, revealing fully formed beans, and should be pliable. The lumpier the pod, the more developed and less tender the bean. A pod that feels dry indicates that the beans are drying out.

Storing: Place the beans in a plastic bag in the refrigerator and use within 3 to 5 days. The natural starches in beans continue to develop after the beans are harvested, diminishing their tenderness and sweetness.

Varieties: pod beans: Blue Lake, haricot vert, Purple King, Romano, yellow wax; shelling beans: black-eyed pea, cranberry, Dragons Tongue, lima, rattlesnake

Three-Bean Soup

Mid- to late summer is the best time of the season to purchase beans when both wax and shell beans are available and at their most tender. Here, a simple soup base of onion, garlic, and fresh tomatoes shows off a trio of summer beans. Serve this simple soup for lunch or dinner. [SERVES 8]

½ pound yellow wax beans

½ pound Romano beans

1 pound cranberry beans

2 tablespoons olive oil

2 cloves garlic, coarsely chopped

½ medium yellow onion, finely chopped

2 medium tomatoes, cored and chopped

2 teaspoons coarse sea salt

2 teaspoons finely chopped mixed fresh herbs such as rosemary, sage, and thyme

2 bay leaves

½ cup elbow macaroni

1. Using fingers, trim the ends of the yellow wax and Romano beans. Cut or break the beans into 1-inch pieces. You should have about 4 cups total. Remove the cranberry beans from the pods.

2. In a large soup pot over medium heat, warm the olive oil. Add the garlic and cook, stirring, until fragrant, about 1 minute. Add the onion and cook, stirring occasionally, until translucent, about 5 minutes. Add the tomatoes and cook, stirring, until the tomatoes are soft and starting to break down. Pour in 6 cups water. Add the salt, herbs, and bay leaves. Raise the heat to high, bring to a boil, and boil the tomato mixture for 20 minutes.

3. Reduce the heat to medium, add the cranberry beans, cover, and cook for 10 minutes. Add the elbow macaroni and the yellow wax and Romano beans. Cover the pot and cook until the noodles are tender, about 10 minutes. Serve immediately.

KIDS CAN
trim the pod beans and break them into pieces • shell the cranberry beans • measure the ingredients for the soup and add to the pot • stir the soup

Berries, Berries, Berries

Summertime is berry time. Berries are great to eat raw or cooked, particularly in fruit desserts and for making jam. At the market, you may find hybrids of blackberries and raspberries such as boysenberries and loganberries. Golden raspberries and black raspberries are often sold only during the peak of the season. Another favorite berry, blueberry, is frequently sold at farmers' markets.

Choosing: Choose plump, shapely berries that are free of mold.

Storing: Berries are fragile and must be handled gently. Arrange them, unwashed, in a single layer in a shallow pan lined with paper towels. Top with a layer of paper towels, then cover the pan with plastic wrap. Refrigerate for up to 2 days. To freeze berries, arrange them in a single layer on a baking sheet and freeze for up to 24 hours. Place the berries in a lock-top freezer bag and freeze for up to 1 year.

Varieties: black raspberry, blueberry, golden raspberry, boysenberry, logan-berry, marionberry, olallieberry

Meringue Shells with Mixed Berries

Homemade meringues offer a bit of sugar-fairy magic for kids. The meringues look fanciful and elegant but are easy to prepare. Fashioned into cuplike shapes and baked to crisp perfection, they serve as bowls for lightly sweetened berries. A combination of berries, in a mixture of colors, makes for a colorful dessert. [SERVES 12 TO 14]

FOR THE MERINGUES

6 egg whites, at room temperature

½ teaspoon salt

1½ teaspoons cream of tartar

1½ cups sugar

FOR THE BERRIES

3 cups mixed berries, such as blackberries, boysenberries, raspberries, and blueberries

¼ cup sugar

KIDS CAN
pick over and rinse the berries • measure the ingredients • stir the berries and sugar together • whip the egg whites • help form and fill the meringue shells

1. Preheat the oven to 250°F. Line a large baking sheet with parchment paper.

2. To make the meringues: In a large bowl, combine the egg whites, salt, and cream of tartar. Using a handheld mixer on high speed, beat the egg whites until they form soft peaks, about 3 minutes. Add the sugar, about ½ cup at a time, and beat until incorporated. Continue to beat until the peaks are dense, glossy, and stiff, 4 to 5 minutes. Be careful not to overbeat the egg whites, or they will deflate.

3. To form each meringue, scoop up about ¾ cup of the egg white mixture and mound it on the baking sheet to make a circle about 3 inches in diameter. With the back of a spoon, make a well in the center of each circle. You should have 12 to 14 circles.

4. Bake until the shells are dry and pale brown, about 1 hour. Turn off the heat and leave the meringues in the oven with the door closed until they are completely cool. This will take at least 2 hours. (The meringues will keep for up to 2 days, in a brown paper bag, folded over at the top, in a dry place.)

5. To prepare the berries: Pick through the berries, discarding any rotten ones. Put the berries in a bowl. Sprinkle with the sugar and gently stir and toss the berries and sugar. Let stand for 15 to 20 minutes.

6. Place each meringue in a shallow bowl. Spoon the berries and some of their juice onto the meringue. Serve immediately.

Berry Blast Refrigerator Jam

The hardest part of making this jam is keeping kids from eating the berries before you get them home from the market. With so many berry varieties to choose from, your kids will have fun mixing and matching—and snacking on—their favorites.

Many jam and jelly recipes call for pectin to thicken the fruit mixture. This recipe relies on the natural pectin released by the berries as they cook. This is an ideal recipe to make when you have a bunch of kids around. They can each have fun taking a turn at stirring the berries. Once the jam is cooked, it can be eaten right away, warm on a slice of buttered toast. Rather than processed in a water bath for cupboard storage, the jam is stored in the refrigerator. The recipe is for a small batch of jam, which cooks fast and is easy for kids to help make. [MAKES FOUR 1-PINT JARS OR EIGHT HALF-PINT JARS]

2½ pounds mixed berries, such as raspberries, boysenberries, and blackberries (about 7 cups; go by weight as types of berries vary in cup amount)

1½ pounds sugar (about 2¼ cups)

1 tablespoon freshly squeezed lemon juice

1. Thoroughly wash four 1-pint or eight half-pint canning jars and their lids and screw bands. Put the jars, lids, and screw bands in a large pot and add water to cover. Bring to a boil and continue to boil for 15 minutes to sterilize the jars, lids, and bands. Turn off the heat and leave the jars in the hot water until ready to use. Place a small plate in the freezer for testing the jam.

2. Pick through the berries, discarding any rotten ones. Put the berries in a large, heavy nonreactive saucepan. Add the sugar and stir to combine. Bring the mixture to a boil over medium heat, stirring constantly until the sugar dissolves. Stir in the lemon juice. Raise the heat if

KIDS CAN
pick over and rinse berries • measure fruit and sugar • squeeze lemon juice • stir fruit and sugar before cooking

necessary to bring the berry mixture to a slow boil. Cook, stirring often with a wooden spoon, until the jam thickens to a nice consistency, 1 to 1½ hours.

3. As the jam cooks, use a large spoon to skim any foam from the surface. To test if the jam has reached the jell point, remove the plate from the freezer, place 1 teaspoon of the jam on the plate, and tip the plate slightly. If the jam does not spread, it is ready. You can also test the jam with a candy thermometer, which will register 220°F when the jam reaches the jell point.

4. Using tongs, lift the jars, lids, and screw bands from the hot water and dry thoroughly. Ladle the jam into the sterilized jars, leaving a ½-inch headspace. Wipe each jar rim clean with a damp towel, then top with a lid and seal tightly with a screw band. Let the jars cool over-night. Label the jars with the recipe name and date (see page 42) and store in the refrigerator for up to 3 months.

Blackberry Tie-Dye T-shirts

Eating berries has led to many accidentally stained T-shirts that look like a Jackson Pollock canvas. There is nothing unintentional about these sassy and stylin' tie-dyes, which hark back to the colorful fashions of the 1960s. You can double the recipe and tell your kids to invite their friends over for an eco-friendly couture event. Dyes made from berries are organic, and the leftovers can be composted. Everyone can wear the shirts to the next farmers' market and show them off. [MAKES 4 DYED SHIRTS]

8 cups blackberries

Cheesecloth

½ cup distilled white vinegar

4 small white T-shirts or tank tops

40 medium rubber bands

KIDS CAN
wrap the rubber bands around the shirts to create designs • remove the rubber bands after the dye is set

1. In a large stockpot, bring 2 quarts water to a boil. Add the berries and reduce the heat to a simmer. Cook for 35 to 40 minutes. Strain the berry mixture through a colander lined with cheesecloth. Return the dye to the pot and stir in the vinegar.

2. Lay a shirt out flat. With an index finger and thumb, pinch the top layer of fabric and pull it up. Begin wrapping a rubber band around this piece of fabric until you have a section of fabric 1 to 3 inches long. Repeat the process to create 10 sections of fabric on each shirt. Be sure to vary the locations, working on the back, sides, and even shoulders of the T-shirts.

3. Bring the dye to a simmer. Add the shirts one at a time and stir them with a wooden spoon to make sure that they are submerged in the dye. (If your pot is too small, you may have to dye the shirts in batches or use two pots.) Let the shirts soak in the simmering dye for at least 1 hour or up to 4 hours for more intense color.

4. Using tongs, remove the shirts from the dye. Squeeze out the extra dye, then remove the rubber bands. Rinse the shirts until the water runs clear and hang to dry. Wash in cold water with like or dark colors; the shirts will fade over time with washing.

Corn

For many market-goers, corn embodies the true taste of summer. With names like Sundance and Silver Queen, corn varieties conjure sun-soaked days. Corn is called a vegetable, but botanically it is a grass. Hundreds of corn varieties, white, yellow, and bicolor, are cultivated. Several types are edible, including sweet corn, waxy corn, flint corn, and popcorn. Sweet corn is the kind most often found on our dinner plates. Most people prefer supersweet corn, which is bred for its high sugar content. At the market, you may see old-fashioned varieties that are not as sweet and thus not commonly available in grocery stores.

Choosing: The ears should be full at the tip, with tightly wrapped, bright-green leaves and pale-yellow silk. The kernels should be tightly packed and spurt "milk" when poked (which you should do if you can!). Corn is too old if the kernels are tough and wrinkled.

Storing: Corn is best eaten the day it is purchased. If you must store the ears, wrap them in plastic bags and keep in the vegetable bin of the refrigerator for up to 2 days. If you haven't cooked the corn after 2 days, cut the kernels from the cobs, place in lock-top freezer bags, and freeze for up to 2 months. The longer fresh corn sits, the more the starches develop, making the corn tough and diminishing the flavor.

Varieties: Butter and Sugar, Silver Queen, Sundance

Perfectly Grilled Corn on the Cob with Chili-Lime Butter

Most kids feel that the best way to eat corn is on the cob. Although grilling the corn is an adult task, your kids can make the flavored butter while you work the grill. If your kids don't like spice, substitute 3 tablespoons chopped basil for the chili powder. [SERVES 6 TO 8]

½ cup salted butter, at room temperature

1 teaspoon mild chili powder or sweet paprika

1 teaspoon grated lime zest

1 tablespoon honey

6 to 8 ears of corn, husks and silk removed

KIDS CAN
husk the corn and remove the silk • grate the lime zest • measure and mix the ingredients for the butter • cut out the parchment paper • roll the butter

1. Cut out a 9-inch square of parchment paper.

2. Place the butter in a small bowl. Add the chili powder, lime zest, and honey. With a wooden spoon, mix the butter and seasonings to soften the butter and evenly distribute the seasonings. Scoop the flavored butter onto the center of the parchment paper. Fold one edge of the paper over the butter, tucking it under the butter. Then use your palms to shape the butter into a smooth, uniform log about 1½ inches in diameter and 6 inches long. Roll up the log in the paper and twist the ends of the paper tightly. Refrigerate the butter for at least 1 hour or up to 24 hours.

3. Prepare a fire in a charcoal or gas grill. Arrange the ears of corn on the grill rack and cook for 5 minutes. Turn the ears and cook until the corn just begins to darken and grill marks appear, about 5 minutes. Rather than grill the ears, you can boil them for 4 to 5 minutes.

4. Cut the butter into ¼-inch-thick rounds. Serve the butter with the piping-hot corn.

Sweet-and-Salty Dried Corn Bites

If your kids like corn nuts, they will adore these sweet-and-salty corn bites. They are easy to make with any variety of fresh corn and are perfect for munching while watching a movie. You will have to cut the kernels from the cobs unless you have an advanced cook in your household, but there is plenty for little hands to do. [MAKES ABOUT 3½ CUPS]

4 ears of corn, husks and silk
  removed

2 tablespoons coarse sea salt

2 tablespoons honey

1. Preheat the oven to 250°F. Line two baking sheets with parchment paper.

2. Using a sharp knife, cut the corn kernels from the cobs. You should have 4 cups. Place the corn in a large bowl.

3. Add the salt and honey and stir gently with your hands to coat the kernels evenly. Divide the kernels between the baking sheets and spread them in a single layer.

4. Bake the kernels until crisp, about 2 hours. Let the kernels cool completely on the baking sheets. The corn bites can be stored in an airtight container at room temperature for up to 3 months.

KIDS CAN
cut parchment paper
for the baking sheets •
husk the corn and remove
the silk • mix the kernels
and seasonings • spread
the kernels on the
baking sheets

Summer Corn Pudding

Kids will enjoy the pillowy texture of this savory pudding. The recipe is quite versatile. You can add herbs such as cilantro or parsley and sautéed summer vegetables such as zucchini and bell peppers. [SERVES 4 TO 6]

2 large ears of corn, husks and silk removed

1 tablespoon unsalted butter

1 shallot, minced

2 teaspoons finely chopped chives

3 eggs

½ teaspoon salt

1 cup grated white Cheddar cheese

3 cups milk

½ cup yellow cornmeal

KIDS CAN
husk the corn and remove the silk • crack the eggs • grate the cheese • measure and mix ingredients • pour the pudding into the baking dish

1. Preheat the oven to 350°F. Butter a deep 8-inch square or round baking dish.

2. Using a sharp knife, cut the corn kernels from the cobs. You should have 1½ to 2 cups.

3. In a large frying pan over medium heat, melt the butter. As the butter begins to foam, add the shallot, corn, and chives and cook, stirring occasionally, until the corn is soft and has released some of its juices, about 5 minutes. Remove from the heat.

4. In a medium bowl, whisk together the eggs and the salt. Stir in the cheese and set aside.

5. In a saucepan, bring 2 cups of the milk to a gentle boil. Whisk the cornmeal into the hot milk and reduce the heat to low. Whisk constantly until the mixture resembles a thick porridge, about 5 minutes. Remove from the heat and whisk in the remaining 1 cup milk, the corn mixture, and the egg mixture. Pour into the baking dish.

6. Bake the pudding until it is lightly golden and a toothpick inserted into the center comes out clean, about 45 minutes. Let the pudding rest for 5 to 10 minutes then scoop into bowls to serve.

Corn Tamale Pie

Rather than prepare tacos for a crowd, you can offer this corn tamale pie—essentially corn bread and Mexican meat loaf in one dish. The pie is fun to prepare when corn is at its peak. Kids will enjoy spooning the cornbread topping over the meat filling and watching it bake to a golden brown. If you like, you can top servings of the pie with sour cream. [SERVES 4 TO 6]

FOR THE FILLING

1 ear of corn, husks and silk removed

1¼ pounds extra-lean ground beef

1 teaspoon salt

2 tablespoons olive oil

¼ cup finely chopped red onion

2 tablespoons finely chopped red bell pepper

2 small red tomatoes, cored and coarsely chopped

2 teaspoons tomato paste

2 teaspoons ground cumin

1. To make the filling: Using a sharp knife, cut the corn kernels from the cob. You should have 1 cup. Warm a 10-inch ovenproof skillet over medium heat. Add the ground beef and salt. Cook, stirring often, until the meat is browned, about 7 minutes. Using a slotted spoon, remove the meat to a plate. Pour off any fat from the skillet. Place the skillet over medium heat and warm the olive oil. Add the onion and cook, stirring often, until soft, about 3 minutes. Add the corn and bell pepper and toss to combine. Stir in the tomatoes, tomato paste, and cumin. Add the cooked beef and stir to combine with the vegetables. Cook, stirring often, until the ingredients are well blended, about 15 minutes. Spread the filling evenly over the bottom of the skillet.

2. Preheat the oven to 375°F.

KIDS CAN
husk the corn and remove the silk • crack the egg • grate the cheese • measure ingredients for the filling and the crust • spread the crust mixture on the pie

FOR THE CRUST

1 cup cornmeal

½ cup all-purpose flour

2 teaspoons baking powder

1 tablespoon sugar

¾ teaspoon salt

1 cup milk

1 egg

2 tablespoons salted butter, melted

½ cup grated Monterey Jack cheese

3. To make the crust: In a medium bowl, combine the cornmeal, flour, baking powder, sugar, and salt. Add the milk and the egg and mix to combine. Add the melted butter and the cheese. Mix well. Evenly spread the cornmeal mixture over the filling in the skillet.

4. Bake until the crust is golden brown, about 20 minutes. Let the pie cool slightly before serving.

Cucumbers

From light yellow to deep sea green, the array of cucumbers at the farmers' market easily exceeds the choices at the grocery store. At summer markets, you might encounter the egg-shaped lemon cucumber; the long, pale-green Armenian variety; and the petite Kirby. There are two basic types: slicing or table cucumbers and pickling cucumbers. Cucumbers are approximately 96 percent water and are refreshing served cold with a sprinkling of salt.

Choosing: For both slicing and pickling cucumbers, choose firm, unblemished specimens. All cucumbers become mealy and bitter when they get too big. The best slicing cucumbers are 5 to 8 inches long. Most pickling cucumbers are less than 5 inches long and have a more tex- tured skin. Look for cucumbers that have a bit of stem attached, as this helps them retain moisture.

Storing: Put cucumbers in a plastic bag and refrigerate for up to 5 days. After that, they will lose their garden-fresh crispness and begin to wilt.

Varieties: Armenian, cornichon, English, Kirby, lemon

PRODUCE OF U.S.A.

Chilled Cucumber and Dill Soup

If your kids think that a cold soup is a funny idea, tell them that they will be making a creamy cucumber smoothie. If you can find seedless cucumbers, use them for this recipe. Otherwise, removing the seeds with a spoon is an easy task for kids. [SERVES 6 TO 8]

1 tablespoon olive oil

½ cup chopped yellow onion

1 teaspoon salt

¼ teaspoon finely ground pepper

1 clove garlic, minced

4 medium cucumbers, preferably seedless, peeled

1 cup sour cream

1 cup nonfat plain yogurt

1 tablespoon freshly squeezed lemon juice

1 tablespoon chopped dill

1. In a small frying pan over medium heat, warm the olive oil. Add the onion and cook, stirring occasionally, until soft, about 3 minutes. Add the salt, pepper, and garlic and continue to cook, stirring occasionally, until fragrant, about 2 minutes. Let cool.

2. If using seedless cucumbers, chop them. If the cucumbers have seeds, cut each one in half lengthwise, scoop out the seeds with the tip of a spoon, and then chop.

3. Working in batches, place the cucumbers, sour cream, yogurt, lemon juice, and cooled onion mixture in a blender or food processor and process until smooth. Pour into a bowl or pitcher. Refrigerate for at least 1 hour or up to 6 hours.

4. To serve the soup, ladle or pour it into bowls. Sprinkle with the chopped dill.

KIDS CAN
rinse and peel the cucumbers • scoop out the seeds if necessary • measure and add ingredients to the blender or food processor • help ladle the soup into bowls

Crunchy Refrigerator Pickles

Ever watch your kids devour a whole jar of pickles in one sitting? Now they can eat as many as they can make with this simple recipe. The pickles, like the jams in this book, are not processed in a hot-water bath and must be stored in the refrigerator.

Cucumbers lose moisture quickly once they are picked, so they need to be soaked in water before pickling to rehydrate them, which helps ensure that the pickles turn out crisp. This means that you will have to start the recipe a day ahead of time. The recipe requires pickling salt, a very fine noniodized salt that is free of additives. The anticaking agents in regular table salt will turn pickled vegetables dark. Using wide-mouth pint jars will make it easier to fill them with cucumbers and pour in the hot brine—and for little hands to remove the pickles. [MAKES SIX 1-PINT JARS]

About 25 blemish-free cucumbers, each 4 to 6 inches long

4 cups water

2 cups cider vinegar

⅓ cup plus 1 tablespoon pickling salt

3 teaspoons brown mustard seeds

1 bunch fresh dill

1. Place the cucumbers in a large bowl and add water to cover by 2 inches or so. Let stand overnight.

2. The next day, thoroughly wash six 1-pint canning jars and their lids and screw bands. Put the jars, lids, and screw bands in a large pot and add water to cover. Bring to a boil and continue to boil for 15 minutes to sterilize the jars, lids, and bands. Turn off the heat and leave the jars in the hot water until ready to use.

KIDS CAN
rinse the cucumbers and check them for soft spots • trim and slice cucumbers • measure the brine ingredients • help put the cucumbers in the jars

3. Pour the 4 cups water into a large nonreactive saucepan. Add the vinegar and pickling salt and bring to a boil over a high heat, stirring to dissolve the salt. Meanwhile, remove the cucumbers from the soaking water. Trim off the tips of each cucumber and cut lengthwise into quarters.

4. Using tongs, lift the jars, lids, and screw bands from the hot water and dry thoroughly. Stand the cucumber quarters upright in the jars; they should fit snuggly. Add ½ teaspoon of the mustard seeds to each jar. Immediately ladle the hot brine into the jars, leaving a ¼-inch headspace. Use a clean skewer or chopstick to tuck sprigs of fresh dill among the cucumbers. Wipe each jar rim clean with a damp towel, then top with a lid and seal tightly with a screw band. Let the jars cool overnight.

5. Label the jars with the recipe name and date (see page 42). The pickles will keep for up to 3 months in the refrigerator.

Melons

Melons belong to the same botanical family as squashes, gourds, and cucumbers. They fall into two broad categories: watermelon and musk-melon. The latter includes cantaloupe, Crenshaw, and honeydew melons. You are sure to find regional varieties of both types at your market: muskmelons that are big or small, round or oblong, with seeds or without, and watermelons that are green, striped, or spotted, with pink, red, or yellow flesh. For a refreshing and handy summertime snack, cut a melon into cubes and keep the cubes in a container in the refrigerator so kids can serve themselves.

Choosing: Look for melons that are evenly shaped and heavy for their size. The rind should be free of blemishes and bruises and should make a deep thud when tapped. A pale-white (but not soft) "ripe spot" on one side where the watermelon lay on the ground indicates that the melon was ripe when picked. Muskmelons should have a noticeably sweet fragrance and give slightly when pressed on both the flower and the stem ends.

Storing: A vine-ripened melon will turn quickly, so eat it within 2 days of purchase. Store whole melons in the refrigerator or in a dark, cool place. Store cut melons in tightly sealed containers (once cut, they release a gas that can spoil other foods) in the refrigerator for up to 3 days.

Varieties: Canary, cantaloupe, Charentais, Crenshaw, honeydew, pink honeydew, Sharlyn

Melon Medley *Paletas*

Paletas are traditional Mexican ice pops, usually made from puréed summer fruits. Melons are especially good for pops because they are naturally high in water and sugar. This recipe calls for watermelon, cantaloupe, and honeydew, but you can experiment with the types of melon available at your market. If you don't have molds, you can use large ice-cube trays or paper cups and wooden ice-pop sticks. The yield is approximate and depends on the size of your melons and your molds. If you have too much fruit purée for the number of molds, you can combine the extra with ice in a blender and make refreshing fruit drinks, called *aguas frescas*, to enjoy before the pops are ready. [MAKES ABOUT 12 *PALETAS*]

1 small seedless watermelon

1 small cantaloupe

1 small honeydew melon

KIDS CAN
scoop the seeds from the melons • remove the melon flesh with an ice-cream scoop • place the melon in the blender and make the purée • help fill the molds

1. Cut each melon in half. With a spoon, scoop out the seeds from the cantaloupe and honeydew. Then scoop out the flesh from all the melons with an ice-cream scoop. Or you can cut the flesh from the rind with a knife, then cut it into chunks.

2. Have ready 12 ice-pop molds. You may want to have more on hand in case you end up with extra purée.

3. Put the watermelon in a blender and process until smooth. Fill one-third of the molds with the purée. Rinse out the blender and repeat with the cantaloupe and then with the honeydew. The purée can be a bit chunky.

4. Place the molds in the freezer. If you are using nontraditional molds, such as ice-cube trays or paper cups, you will need to freeze the purée until it is partially frozen, usually about 2 hours, then insert a stick into each mold and return the molds to the freezer.

5. Freeze the *paletas* for at least 8 hours or up to 24 hours. They will keep in the freezer for 1 week.

Watermelon Gelatin with Summer Berries

Because watermelon, true to its name, is full of water, it is perfect for making this dessert. The mystery of gelatin is fun for kids to observe as they watch it turn from a liquid into the familiar jiggly dessert. You can use a clear glass bowl so that kids can see the berries swimming around in what looks like a big fruit-filled aquarium. When you add the berries to the gelatin mixture is crucial: The mixture must be partially set. If you add them too soon, they will float to the top. [SERVES 6 TO 8]

1 small watermelon, about
   10 pounds

2 packages powdered gelatin

1 tablespoon freshly squeezed
   lemon juice

⅓ cup sugar

1 pint raspberries or blueberries

KIDS CAN
juice the melon •
measure the juice and add
the gelatin • rinse and
pick over the berries •
add the berries to
the gelatin

1. Cut the watermelon in half crosswise. Then cut each half in half. Finally, cut each piece crosswise into triangular-shaped slices. Set a box grater over a large, wide bowl and grate each piece of melon. You can also remove the flesh with an ice-cream scoop, place it in a large bowl, and squeeze out the juice with your hands.

2. Line a colander with cheesecloth and place over a large bowl. Strain the grated melon, pressing on it with a spoon to extract as much juice as possible. Measure 4 cups of juice (set aside any remaining juice for drinking). Put ½ cup of the juice in another large bowl. Sprinkle the gelatin over the juice and let stand. Pour the remaining 3½ cups juice into a medium saucepan and bring to a boil. A red foam of solids will float to the top. Use a large spoon to skim off this foam. Add the lemon juice and sugar and stir until the sugar is dissolved, about 2 minutes. Pour the hot juice over the dissolved gelatin and stir until any lumps have disappeared.

3. Refrigerate the gelatin for 1 hour. It will begin to thicken. Gently place the berries in the gelatin. Using a wooden skewer or the end of a spoon, push the berries below the surface of the gelatin. Return the gelatin to the refrigerator and let it set for at least 6 hours before serving.

Peaches, Nectarines, and Plums

Peaches, nectarines, and plums are all summer stone fruits—fruits with a hard pit at their center that conceals a seed. Peaches and nectarines, with skin in shades of white, yellow, orange, or pink, are technically separated by one gene—the one that makes peach skin fuzzy and nectarine skin smooth. Plums, the gemstones of the family, show up in markets with skin and flesh in pink, scarlet, purple, blue black, green, yellow, or amber jewel tones. You'll sometimes see all three fruits labeled "freestone" or "clingstone." The former are varieties in which the flesh pulls easily away from the pit, and the latter are varieties in which it doesn't. All stone fruits: can be stewed, poached, or used in jellies, jams, sauces, puddings, crisps, cobblers, cakes, and tarts, as well as in savory dishes.

Choosing: Ripe stone fruits should be fragrant and free of bruises or breaks in the skin. A ripe peach should be firm with a bit of give, and nectarines should be firm but not rock hard. Plums, unlike peaches and nectarines, sometimes have a powdery white coating on their skin called bloom—a natural indicator of ripe fruit. Depending on the variety, some ripe plums are firm, and others soft, but you should always pass up a squishy one.

Storing: Keep stone fruits at room temperature until they are fully ripe. Once ripe, they can be refrigerated for 2 days; do not put them in a plastic bag. When picked ripe, stone fruits won't last long. If they start to turn before you have a chance to eat them, make jam or compote. If they are not quite ripe when brought home, place them in a brown paper bag to encourage ripening.

Varieties: nectarines: Fantasia, Flavortop, Ruby Diamond, Summer Fire; peaches: Arctic Supreme, August Lady, Indian Blood, O'Henry, Summerset, Sun Crest; plums: damson, Elephant Heart, Greengage

Tangy Fruit-Leather Rolls

Making these rolls takes time, but the concentrated flavor is so much better than the store-bought version that they are worth it. Unlike most commercial fruit rolls, home-made rolls don't have much sugar, so they are tangy, the way most kids like them. The trick is to have the oven at a low setting and to leave the rolls in the oven for at least 3 hours. This is a good project for days when you have other things to do at home at the same time. The recipe calls for peaches, but you can also try plums, nectarines, or apricots. [MAKES 8 ROLLS]

Cooking spray or vegetable oil
for pan

5 pounds peaches, peeled and
pitted

12 tablespoons freshly squeezed
lemon juice

1 cup water

KIDS CAN
grease the pans • peel the peaches if they are soft enough • break the peaches into chunks • crush the fruit • help spread the purée in the pan • cut and roll the finished leather

1. Preheat the oven to 250°F. Generously coat two rimmed baking sheets with cooking spray or oil.

2. Cut the peaches into 1-inch chunks and place in a large bowl. Use a masher or your hands to crush the peaches into a pulp. Put the peach pulp in a large nonreactive saucepan. Add the lemon juice and the water and stir. Bring to a boil over high heat, reduce the heat to medium, and cook, stirring often, until the peaches are reduced by about one-third, 20 to 30 minutes. The key to making this fruit leather is to cook out as much moisture as possible from the peaches before putting them in the oven. Put the peaches in a food processor or blender and purée until smooth.

3. Pour the purée onto the baking sheets. Using a rubber spatula, spread it evenly into a generous ⅛-inch-thick layer. The layer must be thick enough so that the bottom of the baking sheet is not visible. If the purée is spread too thin, the leather will become crisp and brittle. If it is too thick, it may not fully dehydrate and may stay sticky in spots.

4. Bake until the leather is slightly tacky to the touch but is not wet or crisp, about 3 hours. The timing will depend on the amount of moisture in the purée and how accurately your oven heats to the setting.

5. Remove the pans from the oven. Have ready two sheets of plastic wrap, each slightly larger than the dimensions of the pan. While the leather is still hot, place the sheet over the top of the leather in each pan. Slip one end of the plastic under one edge of the leather and pull the leather from the pan. Let the leather cool until you can handle it. Cut both pieces of leather into four equal rectangles. Place each rectangle on a piece of plastic wrap the same size as the rectangle, and roll the leather. Tie with a piece of kitchen twine. Keep up to 3 months in an airtight container.

Mix-and-Match Deep-Dish Fruit Desserts

Cobblers, slumps or grunts, and pandowdies are all baked deep-dish fruit desserts with a topping. A cobbler is finished with biscuit dough; grunts and slumps, two names for the same dish, are crowned with a dumpling-type topping. They are traditionally cooked on the stovetop but can be baked, as here. A pandowdy sports a thick pastry topping. After it comes out of the oven, the topping is broken up and pushed into the dessert.

This recipe is fun for kids because they can choose one of three toppings: cottage pudding, an old-fashioned batter cake for slumps and grunts; a drop-biscuit dough for cobblers; and a flaky pastry dough for pandowdies. [SERVES 6 TO 8]

FOR THE FILLING

4 pounds peaches, nectarines, or plums

1 teaspoon freshly squeezed lemon juice

2 tablespoons sugar

Cottage Pudding (page 78), Drop Biscuits (page 78), or Flaky Pastry Dough (page 79)

KIDS CAN
rinse and peel the fruit and cut into wedges • measure and mix filling and topping ingredients • help top the filling

1. Preheat the oven to 350°F.

2. To make the filling: If using peaches, peel them. If using nectarines or plums, leave the skin on. Pit the fruits and cut into ½-inch-thick wedges. You should have about 4 cups. Put the wedges in a bowl. Add the lemon juice and sugar and stir and toss to mix well. Put the fruit in a 9-inch round or square baking dish deep enough to hold both the filling and the topping.

3. If using Cottage Pudding or Drop Biscuits, drop the batter by spoonfuls on to the filling, distributing the topping evenly. If using Flaky Pastry Dough, on a lightly floured work surface, roll out the dough ½ inch thick. It should be the shape of the dish—round, square, or rectagular— and just slightly larger than the dish. Drape the dough around the rolling pin and carefully lay it over the filling. Crimp the edges of the dough. Cut a few slits in the top to release steam during baking.

4. Bake until the crust is golden and the fruit is bubbling up around the edges, about 45 minutes. Let cool on a wire rack for 10 to 15 minutes before serving.

Cottage Pudding

1½ cups all-purpose flour

½ cup sugar

2 teaspoons baking powder

½ teaspoon salt

1 egg, well beaten

½ cup milk

½ cup unsalted butter, melted

In a large bowl, sift together the flour, sugar, baking powder, and salt. In a medium bowl, whisk together the egg, milk, and butter until well blended. Gradually add the egg mixture to the flour mixture, stirring gently until fully blended. Proceed as directed in the main recipe.

Drop Biscuits

2 cups all-purpose flour

1 tablespoon baking powder

2 teaspoons sugar

½ teaspoon cream of tartar

¼ teaspoon salt

½ cup unsalted butter, melted

1 cup milk

In a large bowl, stir together the flour, baking powder, sugar, cream of tartar, and salt. Stir in the butter and milk just until the flour mixture is moistened. Proceed as directed in the main recipe.

Flaky Pastry Dough

The key to making the flakiest crust is to work quickly so that the butter remains very cold. You can also use this dough for making turnovers (page 32), two single-crust pies or one double-crust pie, or tartlets (page 127).

2½ cups all-purpose flour

½ teaspoon salt

1 cup cold butter, cut into 1-inch pieces

⅓ cup ice-cold water

In a large bowl, stir together the flour and salt. Scatter the butter over the flour and cut it in with a pastry blender until the mixture resembles coarse sand. Sprinkle the water evenly over the mixture and, using a fork, toss to moisten evenly. Gently press the dough into a ball, then flatten into a disk. Wrap in plastic wrap and chill in the refrigerator for 2 hours (or keep in the freezer for up to 2 months).

Frozen Nectarine Yogurt

Frozen yogurt is easier to make than ice cream because you don't have to prepare a custard base. This recipe uses honey, often sold at farmers' markets, rather than sugar. You'll find a range of flavors, depending on what local pollen the bees collected, such as lavender, orange, heather, or rosemary. Make sure that the nectarines are very ripe and soft.

The frozen yogurt makes a perfect filling for gingersnap cookie sandwiches. Prepare your favorite cookie recipe and make the cookies about 3 inches in diameter. For each sandwich, place about 2 tablespoons frozen yogurt between two baked cookies, arrange the sandwiches on a baking sheet, and freeze until the yogurt is hard, at least 3 hours.

[MAKES ABOUT 1 QUART]

1½ pounds very ripe nectarines, peeled and pitted

1 tablespoon freshly squeezed lemon juice

⅓ cup water

½ cup honey

2 cups vanilla whole-milk yogurt

1. Chop the nectarines and put them in a medium saucepan. Add the lemon juice and the water. Cook over medium heat until the fruit begins to soften, about 20 minutes. Stir in the honey and let the mixture cool to room temperature.

2. Purée the nectarine mixture in a blender or food processor. Pour the purée into a large bowl, cover with plastic wrap, and refrigerate for at least 4 hours or up to overnight.

3. Stir the yogurt into the chilled nectarine purée. Transfer to an ice-cream maker and freeze according to the manufacturer's instructions. Serve immediately for a soft frozen-yogurt treat or transfer to an airtight freezer container and freeze for up to 2 weeks.

KIDS CAN
rinse the nectarines and peel, pit, and chop them • measure the ingredients

Edible Dried-Fruit Bracelets

Inspired by the pastel candy chokers found in sweet shops, these tasty bracelets are fashioned from homemade dried peaches and nectarines. Depending on the season, you could also use cherries or grapes. Once the fruit is dried, it will keep for up to 6 months in the refrigerator. You can also dry the fruit in a dehydrator, if you have one. Making the bracelets using dried fruit is a perfect activity for summer birthday parties or for creating gifts for friends. [MAKES 4 BRACELETS]

6 nectarines, peeled, halved, and pitted

6 peaches, peeled, halved, and pitted

Mini heart-shaped or triangle-shaped cookie cutters

Large embroidery needle

4 pieces of thin kitchen twine, each 8 inches long

1 cup raisins

1. Preheat the oven to 225°F.

2. Cut the nectarine and peach halves into slices about ⅛ inch thick. Use the cookie cutters to cut shapes from the slices. You will get only one or two shapes from each slice. Cut the scraps into ½-inch pieces.

3. Arrange the cut shapes and scraps, not touching and in a single layer, on a nonstick baking sheet. Bake until the fruit is leathery but not crisp, 2 to 3 hours. The timing will depend on the moisture content of the fruit and the accuracy of the oven temperature. Let cool completely.

4. Thread the embroidery needle with the twine. Slide pieces of fruit onto the string, alternating cookie cutter shapes, scrap shapes, and raisins. When each bracelet is long enough to reach around a wrist, remove the needle and tie the twine securely.

KIDS CAN
rinse the fruits and peel and pit them • cut out shapes • string the dried fruits

Summer Squashes

Zucchini is probably the most popular summer squash, but many other types can be found at farmers' markets, including the small, scalloped pattypan; the larger, speckled scallopini; and the curve-necked yellow crookneck. Unlike winter squashes, summer squashes are young squashes with thin skins and seeds that have not yet fully developed. Their soft texture and mild flavor make them ideal for scooping and stuffing as well as for making moist quick breads. Summer squash varieties are quite similar and therefore are largely inter-changeable in recipes.

Choosing: Small squashes tend to be more flavorful than larger ones. As squashes age on the vine, they become pithy and dry, loosing their fresh flavor, so select specimens that are young and not too large. Make sure they are smooth and have a bright color and no brown spots. Check to see that the stem end is intact, which helps lock in the moisture.

Storing: Keep summer squashes in plastic bags in the refrigerator for 3 to 5 days. Do not rinse them first, as moisture will promote rapid decay.

Varieties: pattypan, Raven, Ronde de Nice, scallopini, Starship, sunburst, yellow crookneck, zucchini

Five-Spice Zucchini Bread

Children will love grating the soft zucchini into heaping mounds for this simple spice bread. All the spices can be purchased already ground, but kids can grind whole cloves and cardamom seeds using a mortar and pestle (or a spice grinder if you are pressed for time) and grind whole nutmeg using a nutmeg grater. For an intense vanilla flavor, you can use the seeds scraped from a 3-inch length of vanilla bean in place of the extract. The muffins make welcome gifts: wrap two or three in parchment paper, tie with baker's string, and add a gift tag. [MAKES ONE 9-BY-5-INCH LOAF OR 12 MUFFINS]

2 to 3 small zucchini

1½ cups all-purpose flour

1½ cups sugar

1 teaspoon baking soda

1 teaspoon baking powder

1 teaspoon salt

¼ teaspoon ground nutmeg

1 teaspoon ground cloves

1 teaspoon ground cinnamon

¼ teaspoon ground cardamom

¼ teaspoon ground ginger

½ cup canola oil

2 eggs, beaten

⅓ cup water

1 teaspoon freshly squeezed
   lemon juice

1 teaspoon pure vanilla extract

1 cup chopped walnuts or pecans

1. Preheat the oven to 350°F. Oil one 9-by-5-inch loaf pan or line 12 standard muffin cups with paper liners.

2. Using a box grater, grate the zucchini into fine shreds. You should end up with about 1 cup.

3. In a large bowl, stir together the flour, sugar, baking soda, baking powder, salt, and spices. In a medium bowl, whisk together the canola oil, eggs, water, lemon juice, vanilla, and zucchini. Stir the zucchini mixture into the flour mixture just until combined. Then gently fold in the nuts.

4. Pour the batter into the prepared loaf pan or spoon into the muffin cups. Bake until a toothpick inserted into the center of the loaf or a muffin comes out clean, 25 to 30 minutes for muffins, 50 minutes to 1 hour for a loaf. Let the loaf cool in the pan on a wire rack for about 10 minutes, then unmold. Let the muffins cool completely in the pan before serving.

KIDS CAN
line the muffin cups or oil the pans • grate the zucchini • measure the ingredients • mix the batter

Summer Squash Lasagna

When sliced thin, summer squashes have a noodlelike texture. This lasagna recipe sneaks a little squash into an otherwise beloved dish, especially for picky eaters who may not like squash in other forms. Homemade tomato sauce makes all the difference in the final lasagna, so it's worth taking the time to prepare your own. When cooking lasagna with kids, the fun part is the assembly. You can set out all the components on a table and have the kids work with you in stages, calling out the layers as you go along. [SERVES 8]

3 tablespoons olive oil

1 clove garlic, halved

2 tablespoons coarse sea salt, plus salt for sprinkling

1 pound dried lasagna noodles

2 cups Tomato Sauce from Scratch (page 87) or other high quality tomato sauce

6 to 8 small summer squashes, trimmed and cut lengthwise into ¼-inch-thick slices

One 15-ounce container whole-milk ricotta cheese

2 cups grated mozzarella cheese

¾ cup grated Parmesan cheese

1. Preheat the oven to 400°F. Coat a 9-by-11-inch baking dish with 1 tablespoon of the olive oil. Rub the dish with the garlic halves, then break up the garlic and leave the pieces in the bottom of the dish.

2. Bring a large pot of water to a rolling boil. Add the sea salt and the lasagna, stir well, and cook until al dente, according to the package directions. Drain the noodles, put in a bowl, and toss them with 1 tablespoon of the olive oil to keep them from sticking together.

3. Set up a workstation with the noodles, sauce, squash slices, and cheeses laid out for assembly. Ladle ½ cup of the sauce into the dish and spread it to coat the bottom evenly. Arrange a layer of noodles, side by side but not overlapping, over the sauce. Top the noodles with ½ cup sauce, again spreading it evenly. Arrange one-third of the squash slices on the sauce in a single layer. Sprinkle the squash with a little salt. Using a tablespoon, dot the squash layer evenly with one-third of the ricotta and sprinkle with one-third of the mozzarella.

4. Repeat the layers of noodles, sauce, squash, ricotta, and mozzarella two more times. Sprinkle the top layer with the Parmesan and drizzle with the remaining 1 tablespoon olive oil.

5. Bake the lasagna until the edges are bubbling and the top is golden brown, about 45 minutes. Let rest for 5 to 10 minutes before serving.

Tomatoes

Many market stands showcase a kaleido-scope of deep orange, yellow, green, pink, dark red, and blackish purple tomato varieties ranging in size from the tiny Sweet 100, just barely ½ inch in diameter, to the huge, misshapen Marvel Stripe, with its marbling of pink and bright orange and its firm, dense flesh. There are 7,500 to 10,000 tomato varieties. The farmers' market is the best place to load up on peak-of-the-season tomatoes, especially local variet-ies that you won't find elsewhere.

Choosing: A ripe tomato should be firm to the touch but not hard and free of soft spots, bruising, or splits in the skin.

Storing: Keep tomatoes at room temperature and eat them as soon as possible after purchase. Refrigerated tomatoes will lose flavor and texture. The exception is a cut tomato, which should be wrapped in plastic wrap and refrigerated. Whole tomatoes can be frozen for up to 1 year. Tomatoes that start to turn soft can be made into sauce.

Varieties: Black Krim, Early Girl, Golden Jubilee, Green Zebra, Marvel Stripe, Roma, Sun Gold, Sweet 100

Tomato Sauce from Scratch

This rich, roasted tomato sauce is easy and satisfying to make with kids. Peeling the boiled tomatoes is both messy and fun—just be sure to let the tomatoes cool long enough so they are safe to handle. Early Girl, Golden Jubilee, and Roma tomatoes are excellent choices for sauce, but any variety will work if you cook them long enough to extract the water. [MAKES ABOUT 4 CUPS]

5 pounds tomatoes

6 cloves garlic, coarsely chopped

¼ cup olive oil

1 teaspoon sea salt

2 teaspoons dried oregano or
   4 fresh oregano sprigs

KIDS CAN
stem the tomatoes • peel the skins from the cooled tomatoes • mash the tomatoes • stir together the tomatoes and other ingredients in the roasting pan

1. Preheat the oven to 300°F.

2. Bring a large pot of water to a gentle boil. Using a paring knife, cut a 1-by-1-inch X just through the skin on the bottom of each tomato. Working in batches, slowly lower the tomatoes into the boiling water. Cook the tomatoes until the skin just begins to pull away from the X, about 1 minute. Using a slotted spoon, remove the tomatoes from pot and place them on a baking sheet to cool. Peel the skins from the cooled tomatoes and cut out the cores. Place the tomatoes in a large bowl and squish them with your hands to make a chunky purée.

3. Pour the tomato purée into a shallow roasting pan. Stir in the garlic, olive oil, salt, and oregano. Roast the purée, stirring occasionally, until it is reduced by at least one-third, about 1½ to 2 hours. Let cool.

4. The sauce will keep in the refrigerator in an airtight container for up to 1 week. To freeze the sauce, put 1-cup portions into lock-top freezer bags. The sauce can be frozen for up to 1 year.

Tomato and Mozzarella Pizza

Prepared-from-scratch tomato sauce makes these pizzas special. Kids can help knead the dough. Then, when it's time to top the pizzas, they can arrange their favorite ingredients, like cooked sausage, sliced mushrooms, or salami, over the sauce. *Bocconcini* are small balls of mozzarella cheese. If you cannot find them, use another type of mozzarella. And if you don't have time to make homemade dough, you can buy pizza dough at many markets in the refrigerated section. [MAKES TWO 12-INCH OR FOUR 6-INCH PIZZAS; SERVES 4]

FOR THE DOUGH

2 envelopes (2¼ teaspoons each)
   active dry yeast

1 cup warm water (105°F)

1 teaspoon sugar

1 teaspoon salt

2 tablespoons olive oil

About 3½ cups all-purpose flour

2 tablespoons cornmeal for pan

4 to 5 tablespoons olive oil

1½ to 2 cups Tomato Sauce from
   Scratch (page 87) or other
   high-quality tomato sauce

2 cups *bocconcini* (about 14 ounces)
   or mozzarella cheese cut into
   1-inch cubes

½ cup basil leaves

1. To make the dough: In a small bowl, dissolve the yeast in the warm water. Add the sugar. Let the mixture stand until it is foamy, about 5 minutes.

2. If making the dough in a food processor, combine the yeast mixture, the salt, 1 tablespoon of the olive oil, and 3 cups of the flour in the processor. Pulse until the ingredients come together into a ball. If the dough is too wet, add more flour, a little at a time, and pulse until the dough has a smooth, firm texture. Continue to process until the dough is smooth and silky but not firm, 3 to 4 minutes longer. Turn the dough out onto a well-floured work surface. Knead the dough until it is elastic, 4 to 5 minutes. Shape it into a ball.

3. If making the dough by hand, in a bowl, combine the yeast mixture, the salt, 1 tablespoon of the olive oil, and 2 cups of the flour. With a fork or your fingertips, work the ingredients together. Gradually add more flour until the dough forms a stiff ball. Turn the dough out onto a well-floured work surface. Knead the dough until it is smooth and elastic, 6 to 7 minutes. Shape it into a ball.

continued

4. Oil a large bowl with the remaining 1 tablespoon olive oil. Place the dough ball in the bowl and turn the ball to coat the surface with oil. Cover the bowl with a kitchen towel and let stand in a warm place until the dough has doubled in size, 1 to 1½ hours. Punch down the dough in the bowl, cover with the towel, and let rest for 30 minutes.

5. Preheat the oven to 500°F.

6. Divide the dough into two or four equal portions, depending on the number of pizzas you are making. On a lightly floured work surface, roll out each portion into a round about ⅛ inch thick. If you are making two pizzas, each round should be about 12 inches in diameter. If you are making four pizzas, each round should be about 6 inches in diameter. Sprinkle two 12-inch pizza pans (if making two large pizzas) or two large rimmed baking sheets (if making two large or four small pizzas) with the cornmeal and put the dough rounds on the pans.

7. Drizzle 2 to 2½ tablespoons olive oil over the dough rounds, dividing the oil evenly. Using a soupspoon, ladle the sauce onto the pizzas, ¾ cup for a large round and ½ cup for a small round. Spread the sauce over the round to within ¼ inch of the edge. Top the pizzas with the *bocconcini*, dividing them evenly.

8. Bake the pizzas until the cheese melts and the crust is just browned at the edges, about 10 minutes for the small pizzas, 15 minutes for the large pizzas.

9. Remove the pizzas from the oven. Drizzle them with the remaining 2 to 2½ tablespoons olive oil and sprinkle with the basil. Cut the large pizzas into wedges and leave the small pizzas whole to serve.

Peak-of-the-Season Tomato Ketchup

Adults love ketchup with their burgers. Kids love burgers with their ketchup. Choose the ripest tomatoes you can find (avoiding the bruised ones) to make this yummy ketchup, which is good with much more than burgers. Try it on fries, hot dogs, and scrambled eggs. Experiment with heirloom tomatoes, such as Green Zebra, Black Krim, or Marvel Stripe, to create colorful ketchups to offer as gifts. Don't hesitate to add more mustard or cinnamon for extra zing. This homemade ketchup has a thinner consistency than the commercial versions, but it is super flavorful. [MAKES FOUR ½-PINT JARS]

5 pounds very ripe tomatoes

¾ pound yellow onions

10 cloves garlic, chopped

1 cup white wine vinegar

Grated zest and juice of ¼ lemon

¾ cup firmly packed brown sugar

1½ teaspoons salt

1½ teaspoons mustard seeds

1 tablespoon peppercorns

1 tablespoon coriander seeds

1 teaspoon whole cloves

1 cinnamon stick, about 1 inch long

1-inch piece fresh ginger, peeled

1. Bring a large pot of water to a gentle boil. Using a paring knife, cut a 1-by-1-inch X just through the skin on the bottom of each tomato. Working in batches, slowly lower the tomatoes into the boiling water. Cook the tomatoes until the skin just begins to pull away from the X, about 1 minute. Using a slotted spoon, remove the tomatoes from pot and put them in a colander to cool. Peel the skins from the cooled tomatoes and cut out the cores. Cut each tomato in half crosswise. Holding each tomato half cut-side down over the sink, squeeze it gently to force out the seeds. If necessary, use a fingertip to coax out the seeds.

2. In a nonreactive saucepan over medium heat, combine the tomatoes, onions, garlic, ½ cup of the vinegar, and the lemon zest and juice. Cook, stirring frequently, until the tomatoes and onions are soft and tender, 15 to 20 minutes.

continued

KIDS CAN

stem and peel the
tomatoes • squeeze the
seeds from the tomatoes •
zest and juice the lemon •
measure the ingredients •
make the spice pouch •
help stir the pot

3 . Remove from the heat and let cool slightly. Working in batches, purée the tomato mixture in a blender or food processor. In the same saucepan, combine the tomato purée, brown sugar, salt, and the remaining ½ cup vinegar. Place the mustard seeds, peppercorns, coriander seeds, cloves, cinnamon stick, and ginger in the center of an 8-inch square of cheesecloth. Gather the corners together and tie securely with kitchen string to make a spice pouch. Add to the tomato mixture.

4 . Place the pan over low heat and bring to a simmer, stirring occasionally. Continue to simmer the tomato mixture, uncovered and stirring occasionally to prevent scorching, until the ketchup is nicely thickened, about 2 hours. Remove from the heat, and remove and discard the spice bag.

5 . Meanwhile, thoroughly wash four ½–pint canning jars and their lids and screw bands. Put the jars, lids, and screw bands in a large pot and add water to cover. Bring to a boil and continue to boil for 15 minutes to sterilize the jars, lids, and bands. Turn off the heat and leave the jars in the hot water until ready to use.

6 . Using tongs, lift the jars, lids, and screw bands from the hot water and dry thoroughly. Ladle the ketchup into the jars, leaving a ½-inch headspace. Wipe each jar rim clean with a damp towel, then top with a lid and seal tightly with a screw band. Let the jars cool overnight. Label the jars with the recipe name and date (see page 42) and store in the refrigerator for up to 3 weeks.

FALL

As summer begins to wane and the days shorten, the fall market bursts with the last produce from the summer harvest and the first evidence of fall: apples, winter squashes, pears, and grapes. By late October, the colors of the market change from sun-drenched reds, sunny yellows, bright greens, and vibrant purples to dusky oranges, chestnut browns, mustard yellows, and dark greens. Come home with nuts for making your own granola, pumpkins for carving into lanterns, apples for baking crisps, and grapes for turning into jelly.

Apples

Some apple varieties are better for eating, and others for cooking. Tart apples, including Newtown Pippin, Sierra Beauty, and Pink Pearl—with its lovely pink-streaked flesh—make good fillings for pies. Sweeter varieties, such as most yellow Delicious apples, are wonderful raw. Many apples—the juicy, mildly tart Baldwin, the aromatic, white-fleshed Jonathan, the diminutive, glossy red-and-yellow Lady—are also labeled "all-purpose" and therefore are good for both cooking or eating raw.

Choosing: Look for fruits that are smooth and firm and free of bruises or brown spots.

Storing: If using the apples within a few days of purchase, leave them at room temperature. Otherwise, store them in plastic bags in the coldest part of the refrigerator. They will keep well for up to 3 weeks.

Varieties: Arkansas Black, Baldwin, Braeburn, Empire, Fuji, Golden Delicious, Granny Smith, Gravenstein, Honeycrisp, Jonathan, Lady, Melrose, Newtown Pippin, Pink Pearl, Sierra Beauty, Winesap, Yellow Bellflower, York Imperial

Mix-and-Match Apple Desserts

Like the cobblers, pandowdies, and slumps in this book made with summer fruits, these crisps, crumbles, and pies featuring a versatile apple filling are simple baked desserts. The crisp and crumble are both crowned with light, flaky toppings—the former with a classic combination of butter and flour, the latter with a robust pairing of walnuts and oats. The same filling can be baked into a double-crust pie. The filling calls for an optional quince—a fragrant, tart relative of the apple. If you can't find it, substitute another apple.

[SERVES 6 TO 8]

FOR THE FILLING

6 apples, peeled, halved, cored, and thinly sliced lengthwise

1 quince, peeled, halved, cored, and cut into ½-inch cubes (see headnote)

1 cup cranberries

½ cup sugar

1 teaspoon ground cinnamon

¼ teaspoon ground cloves

¼ cup freshly squeezed lemon juice

Flaky Pastry Dough (page 79), Crisp Topping (page 100), or Crumble Topping (page 100)

1 tablespoon cold unsalted butter

1. Preheat the oven to 350°F. Have ready a 9-inch pie dish or comparable baking dish.

2. To make the filling: Put the apple slices, quince cubes, and cranberries in a large bowl. Add the sugar, cinnamon, cloves, and lemon juice. Toss to mix well.

continued

KIDS CAN
mix the fruit filling • measure the ingredients for the crisp or crumble topping • help mix the topping and scatter on the fruit • help mix the pie dough and roll out the dough

3. If using the Flaky Pastry Dough, on a lightly floured work surface, roll out each dough disk into a round about 12 inches in diameter and ¼ inch thick. Drape one round over the rolling pin and carefully lay it over the pie dish. Gently ease it into the bottom and sides of the dish. Trim the overhang to about 1 inch. Pour in the apple filling. Brush the rim of the dough with water. Lay the remaining dough round over the pie dish. Trim the overhang to about ½ inch, then fold the edge of the bottom round over the edge of the top round. Crimp the edges with a fork. Cut four or five slits in the top so steam can escape during baking.

If using the Crisp Topping or Crumble Topping, pour the apple filling into the baking dish. Cut the butter into small pieces and dot them over the filling. Scatter the topping mixture evenly over the filling.

4. Bake until the top is golden brown and the fruit is bubbling, 45 minutes to 1 hour. Let cool on a wire rack before serving.

Crisp Topping

1 cup all-purpose flour

½ teaspoon salt

½ cup sugar

½ cup cold unsalted butter,
  cut into ½-inch pieces

In a medium bowl, stir together the flour, salt, and sugar. Scatter the pieces of butter over the top. Using your fingers, blend the ingredients until the mixture is crumbly and the pieces of butter are the size of small peas. Proceed as directed in the main recipe.

Crumble Topping

¾ cup all-purpose flour

½ teaspoon salt

½ cup firmly packed brown sugar

½ cup chopped walnuts

½ cup steel-cut oats

½ cup cold unsalted butter,
  cut into ½-inch pieces

In a medium bowl, stir together the flour, salt, brown sugar, walnuts, and oats. Scatter the pieces of butter over the top. Using your fingers, blend the ingredients until the mixture is the consistency of coarse crumbs. Proceed as directed in the main recipe.

Smooth and Creamy Apple Butter

Apple butter is a spicy, creamier version of applesauce that is used for spreading on toast and topping hot cereal or yogurt. Patience and attentiveness are key to making this slow-cooked spread. The butter will take about 1½ hours to cook. During this time, you and your kids can take turns stirring it, with your supervision. Although making the butter is time-consuming, it will fill your kitchen with the homey aroma of cooked apples and spice. Tart apples are best for this recipe, so ask a vendor at your farmers' market to suggest local varieties. [MAKES 4 HALF-PINT JARS]

4 pounds apples

½ cup apple cider vinegar

Zest and juice of 1 lemon

2½ cups water

2 to 3 cups sugar

1 teaspoon ground cinnamon

1 cinnamon stick, about
   3 inches long

½ teaspoon ground cloves

½ teaspoon salt

1. Cut the apples lengthwise into quarters. Do not peel them or remove the cores. Put the apples in a large nonreactive pot. Add the vinegar and lemon zest and juice. Pour in the water. Bring to a boil over high heat, reduce the heat to low, cover, and simmer until the apples are soft, about 20 minutes. Remove from the heat and let cool.

2. Pour the apples into a food processor and process until they are broken down but still a bit chunky, about 30 seconds. Place a medium-mesh sieve over a bowl. Working in batches, press the apple mixture through the sieve. Discard the pulp. Measure the apple mixture and place in the pot. For each 1 cup of apple mixture, stir in ½ cup sugar. Stir in the ground cinnamon, cinnamon stick, cloves, and salt. Bring to a boil over medium heat and then reduce the heat to a simmer. Place a small dish in

KIDS CAN
rinse and cut the apples • push the cooked apples through the sieve • measure the ingredients and add to the pot • stir the butter as it cooks • help fill the jars

continued

the freezer for testing the butter. Cook the apple mixture, stirring often, until it is reduced by half, 1 to 1½ hours. It is important to stir often so that the apple butter will not stick to the bottom of the pot. The butter will become a rich dark brown and have a somewhat creamy texture.

3. Meanwhile, thoroughly wash four half-pint canning jars and their lids and screw bands. Put the jars, lids, and screw bands in a large pot and add water to cover. Bring to a boil and continue to boil for 15 minutes to sterilize the jars, lids, and bands. Turn off the heat and leave the jars in the hot water until ready to use.

4. Remove the plate from the freezer, place 1 teaspoon of the butter on the plate, and tip the plate slightly. If the butter does not spread, it is ready.

5. Using tongs, lift the jars, lids, and screw bands from the hot water and dry thoroughly. Ladle the apple butter into the jars, leaving a ¼-inch headspace. Wipe each jar rim clean with a damp towel, then top with a lid and seal tightly with a screw band. Let cool overnight. Label the jars with the recipe name and date (see page 42) and store in the refrigerator for up to 1 month.

Pears

At farmers' markets, you might notice two main types of pears. European pears include familiar varieties like Bartlett and Anjou; the firm Bosc, which is perfect for poaching; and the Comice, whose flesh has a smooth, buttery texture. The small and delicate Seckel seems made for children's small hands. Asian pears, also known as apple pears, are crisp and round like apples. The popular Shinko and other varieties are excellent eaten out of hand or added to fruit salads or green salads.

Choosing: European pears ripen off the tree, so choose fruits that are mature but still firm, and let them ripen at room temperature. A ripe pear ready for snacking will have a sweet, fruity fragrance and be slightly firm to the bite. Avoid purchasing pears with bruises or spots or those that are too soft to the touch. Asian pears are harvested when ripe and should be firm when eaten.

Storing: A ripe pear will not last much more than a couple of days. If your pears are still too hard when purchased, slip them in a paper bag and place in a cool, dark place. Asian pears have a longer shelf life than European pears and will keep for 1 week or so at room temperature. They can also be stored in a plastic bag in the refrigerator.

Varieties: Anjou, Bartlett, Bosc, Comice, Golden Russet Bosc, Hosui, Seckel, Shinko, Taylor's Gold, Warren

Poached Pears with Mexican Chocolate Sauce

The fragrant chocolate sauce, spiced with cinnamon and chile, pairs perfectly with the sweet, cooked pears in this dessert that appeals to both kids and adults. Arranging the poached pears is part of the fun of making the recipe. Each pear is served upright in a shallow bowl and accented with a scoop of ice cream, then both are drizzled with the chocolate sauce. Children will enjoy presenting their creations to everyone. When choosing pears, look for firm varieties like Bosc that will hold their shape when poached. [SERVES 6]

1¼ cups sugar

2 tablespoons balsamic vinegar

1 cinnamon stick, about 3 inches long

½ vanilla bean, split lengthwise, or 1 teaspoon pure vanilla extract

Grated zest of 1 lemon

4 cups water

6 firm but ripe pears, with stems intact, peeled

1. In a saucepan large enough to hold the pears, combine the sugar, vinegar, cinnamon stick, vanilla, and lemon zest. Pour in the water and bring to a boil over medium-high heat, stirring constantly until the sugar is dissolved and the spices are fragrant. Remove from the heat.

2. Trim about ¼ inch off the base of each pear to create a flat bottom. Return the poaching liquid to a gentle boil. Using tongs, gently lower the pears into the liquid. Reduce the heat to a simmer and poach the pears, uncovered, turning them occasionally with a wooden spoon so that they cook evenly. The pears are ready when they are easily pierced with a thin skewer. This will take 10 to 20 minutes, depending on the ripeness of the pears. Using a slotted spoon, remove the pears from the pot and place on a large plate. Discard the poaching liquid.

continued

FOR THE CHOCOLATE SAUCE

4 ounces bittersweet chocolate, chopped

¼ cup heavy cream

½ teaspoon ground cinnamon

1 teaspoon pure vanilla extract

¼ teaspoon ancho chile powder

1 tablespoon sugar

1 pint vanilla ice cream

3. To make the chocolate sauce: Combine the chocolate and cream in a heatproof bowl. Place the bowl over (but not touching) barely simmering water in a saucepan. Stir constantly until the chocolate is melted and the mixture is smooth. Add the cinnamon, vanilla, chile powder, and sugar. Continue to stir until the spices are well blended into the chocolate mixture. Remove from the heat.

4. Place the pears in shallow bowls. Add a scoop of ice cream to each bowl. Ladle a spoonful of warm chocolate sauce over the pear and another over the ice cream.

KIDS CAN
rinse the pears • measure the ingredients • test the pears for doneness • ladle the chocolate sauce for serving

Grapes

The grape varieties you find at farmers' markets will depend on those cultivated in your region. These may include Thompson seedless, Flame Red, or Champagne—or such special varieties as Bronx. Old-fashioned grapes like Concord usually have seeds and make especially good jelly. Seedless varieties are better for salads and other dishes.

Choosing: Look for firm, plump fruits and pass up bunches with wrinkled or soft grapes. The greener the stem, the fresher the grapes. Another indicator of freshness is the presence of a harmless white powder called bloom. Fully ripe green grapes will have a yellow cast with a touch of amber rather than be an opaque grassy green. Red grapes should be deep crimson, not a milky or pale red. Blue grapes should be dark, almost black, not pale or tinged with green.

Storing: Check bunches for spoiled grapes and remove them. Store in an open plastic bag in the refrigerator for up to 1 week. Rinse the grapes just before serving. To freeze grapes, divide bunches into small clusters, arrange in a single layer on a baking sheet, freeze, and put in a tightly sealed container. Freeze for up to 1 year.

Varieties: Black Corinth, Bronx, Champagne, Concord, Flame Red, Flame Seedless, Muscadine, Ruby Seedless, Thomcord, Thompson Seedless

Old-Fashioned Grape Jelly

Your peanut butter and jelly sandwiches will never be the same after you make this grape jelly. Because Concord grapes are cultivated primarily for jelly and juice, they are rarely found fresh at grocery stores. They are, however, readily available in farmers' markets. You can make this jam with other grapes, but the Concord's dark-purple skin makes a beautiful jewel-toned jelly. You can also use Thomcord grapes, a seedless hybrid of Thompson and Concord.

The crushed and cooked grapes must be strained to remove the pulp. This is traditionally done with a jelly bag, a reusable muslin or nylon bag that you attach to a metal stand. The stand suspends the bag over a bowl, so that the juice can drip undisturbed, creating a nice clear jelly. Because this is time-consuming, the recipe here offers the option of pushing the grape juice through the jelly bag or through cheesecloth. The jelly will be smooth but somewhat opaque. Grapes are a low-pectin fruit and need more sugar than other fruits to reach the jell point. This recipe is quite sweet, but the jelly sets within several hours. Feel free to experiment with low-sugar pectins.

Although making the jelly takes time, kids like crushing the grapes, watching the juice slowly drip into the bowl, and seeing it jell. [MAKES 9 HALF-PINT JARS]

6 pounds grapes, removed from
    stems

1½ cups water

One 1¾-ounce envelope pectin
    such as Sure-Jell

7 cups sugar

1. Thoroughly wash nine half-pint canning jars and their lids and screw bands. Put the jars, lids, and screw bands in a large pot and add water to cover. Bring to a boil and continue to boil for 15 minutes to sterilize the jars, lids, and bands. Turn off the heat and leave the jars in the hot water until ready to use.

2. Put the grapes in a large nonreactive pot and gently crush them with your hands. Add the water and place the pot over medium heat. Cook, stirring occasionally, until the grapes are very soft and have released their juice, 15 to 20 minutes. Let cool.

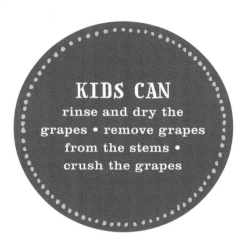

KIDS CAN
rinse and dry the grapes • remove grapes from the stems • crush the grapes

3. Dampen a jelly bag (see headnote), attach it to its stand, and place over a large bowl. Or dampen a double layer of cheesecloth, line a colander, and place over a large bowl. Put the cooled grapes into the bag or the lined colander and let the juice drain into the bowl. To help the juice along, push on the pulp with a wooden spoon. You should have 5 cups of juice. If you have more, pour the juice into the pot and cook it over high heat until reduced to 5 cups. If you have less than 5 cups, add water and pour the juice into the pot.

4. Using tongs, lift the jars, lids, and screw bands from the hot water and dry thoroughly. Add the pectin to the pot and stir until it is dissolved. Bring the juice mixture to a rapid boil and stir in the sugar all at once. Stir constantly for 1 minute. Remove from the heat and immediately ladle the mixture into the jars, leaving a ¼-inch headspace. Wipe each jar rim clean with a damp towel, then top with a lid and seal tightly with a screw band. Let cool overnight at room temperature.

5. Label the jars with the recipe name (see page 42) and date and refrigerate. The jelly will keep for up to 3 months in the refrigerator.

For longer storage, process the jars in a hot-water bath. For the safest method, use a pot intended for canning that has a rack; this keeps the jars stable and allows the water to circulate around the jars. You will also want canning tongs for lowering the jars into the hot water and removing them. Bring a large pot of water to a boil. Using canning tongs, lower the jars into the boiling water. Process the jars in batches if necessary, as they should not touch. They should be submerged by 1½ to 2 inches. Let the water return to a boil and boil the jars for 5 minutes. Turn off the heat and remove the jars from the pot. Let them sit undisturbed for 24 hours until the seal lids invert. The processed jelly will keep in a cool, dry place for up to 1 year.

Grape and Walnut Salad

Sweet, juicy grapes and toasted nuts tossed with soft, tender leaves of butter lettuce combine into a salad that everyone at the table will enjoy. Seedless grapes are ideal for salads, and you can let your kids choose from the varieties at the market. If your farmers' market has a cheese vendor, you may find the perfect fresh goat cheese or other soft cheese for this salad. You can use almonds, pecans, or another variety of nuts in place of the walnuts. [SERVES 4 TO 6]

½ cup walnut halves, coarsely chopped

FOR THE DRESSING

2 tablespoons extra-virgin olive oil

¼ teaspoon salt

½ teaspoon finely chopped shallot

2 teaspoons Champagne vinegar or white wine vinegar

1 head butter lettuce, torn into bite-size pieces

1 cup red or green seedless grapes, cut in half lengthwise

¼ cup soft, young goat cheese, crumbled

1. Preheat the oven to 350°F. Place the walnuts on a baking sheet and toast until they just begin to turn brown and are fragrant, 5 to 7 minutes. Transfer them onto a small plate to cool.

2. To make the dressing: In a medium bowl, combine the olive oil, salt, shallot, and vinegar. Whisk until the salt dissolves.

3. Add the lettuce, grapes, and walnuts to the bowl. Toss to coat the ingredients evenly with the dressing. Sprinkle with the crumbled cheese before serving.

KIDS CAN rinse and dry the lettuce • tear the leaves • wash, pick over, and halve the grapes • measure and mix the ingredients for the dressing • toss the salad and sprinkle with the cheese

Dried-and-True Homemade Raisins

Grapes ripen at the very end of summer and into the fall. Early ripening grapes, if left alone, will shrivel and darken on the vine, resulting in raisins! You can build a simple drying rack so that your kids can watch this miracle of evaporation. Older kids can help you assemble the rack. The grapes are dried outdoors, so be sure to keep the rack away from squirrels and birds. If wildlife are persistent, you can protect the grapes with a net cover. Using small grapes helps cut down on the drying time, which can take up to 1 week for large grapes. [MAKES ABOUT 2 CUPS]

Four 18-inch lengths of 1-by-1-inch pine

Heavy-duty staple gun and staples

One 19-inch square of lightweight non-galvanized wire mesh

Two 3-foot-square pieces of cheesecloth

3 pounds small seedless grapes, stems removed

KIDS CAN
rinse the grapes and remove them from the stems • help build the rack • arrange the grapes on the rack

1. Arrange the pieces of wood in a square. Using the staple gun, secure the pieces with two or three staples on either side of each joint and on the ends. Lay the mesh square over the frame and staple it in place every 2 inches or so around the entire frame.

2. Lay a piece of cheesecloth over the rack. Arrange the grapes, not touching, in a single layer on the cheesecloth. Lay the second piece of cheesecloth over the grapes.

3. Put the rack in the sun. Bring it inside at night to avoid evening and early-morning moisture, then return it to the sunshine. Check daily to see if the grapes are shrinking and drying out. They should be ready in 4 to 7 days, depending on the intensity of the sun. Taste them to check if they are ready. The raisins will keep up to 4 months in an air-tight container.

Nuts

A nut is technically a seed that is also the fruit of a plant. Almonds and walnuts, for example, are both seeds and fruits contained within shells. You can cook with nuts year-round, but nuts are especially good right after the fall harvest. Freshly shelled walnuts can be added to back-to-school granola, and fresh almonds can be ground up to make cookies. Although some recipes here call for specific nuts, most nuts can be substituted for each other.

Choosing: If buying nuts in the shell, check that the shells are firm, with no sign of cracks or mold. The nuts should also feel heavy for their size. If they are light, the nut meats inside are dry. You can shake the nuts, too. If you hear a rattle, pass them up. If buying shelled nuts, look for nuts that are big and plump and not mealy.

Storing: Nuts in the shell should be stored in an airtight container in a cool, dark place, where they will keep for up to 2 months. They can be frozen for up to 6 months.

Varieties: almonds, hazelnuts, pecans, walnuts

Nutty Cookies

These crispy little cookies feature the buttery flavor of fall nuts. The recipe is also a great way to use the nut meal left over from making nut milk. The cookies are delicious simply served with milk. They can also be filled with a favorite homemade jam to make sandwiches. Place a teaspoonful of jam between the undersides of two cookies and gently press them together until the jam oozes to the edges. [MAKES 24 COOKIES]

1½ cups almonds, hazelnuts, or walnuts, or 1 cup almond meal from nut milk (see page 120)

⅔ cup sugar

1½ cups all-purpose flour

½ teaspoon salt

¾ cup cold unsalted butter, cut into small pieces

1 egg yolk

½ teaspoon pure vanilla extract

½ teaspoon almond extract

1. Preheat the oven to 350°F. Line two baking sheets with parchment paper.

2. In a food processor, combine the nuts and the sugar and pulse until finely ground. Add the flour and salt and pulse until blended. Add the butter and pulse just until a sticky paste forms; do not overprocess the mixture. Add the egg yolk, vanilla, and almond extract and pulse until just combined. Gather the dough into a ball and shape it into a thick log. Wrap the dough in plastic wrap and refrigerate for at least 1 hour.

3. Use a serrated knife to slice the dough into ¼-inch rounds. Arrange the rounds on the baking sheets. Bake one sheet at a time until the cookies are just golden brown, approximately 15 minutes. Transfer the cookies to a wire rack to cool completely. Keep the cookies in an airtight container for 3 days or in the refrigerator for 1 week.

KIDS CAN
measure the ingredients • help pulse them in the food processor • shape the dough • roll the dough into a log • slice the dough

Cinnamon-Nut Swirl Monkey Bread

It isn't clear how monkey bread got its name, but the other name for the bread, pinch-me cake, more accurately describes how many people like to eat it. Made of pieces of rolled sweet dough, the segments of baked bread can be pinched from the loaf and eaten with your fingers. The layers of dough are interspersed with ground nuts, sugar, and cinnamon. This breakfast treat is especially fun for kids to prepare and eat. [MAKES ONE 10-INCH LOAF]

1½ cups milk

½ cup unsalted butter

⅓ cup sugar, plus a pinch

1 package (2¼ teaspoons) active dry yeast

¼ cup warm water (80° to 85°F)

4¼ cups all-purpose flour

1½ teaspoons salt

FOR THE TOPPING

1½ cups almonds, hazelnuts, or walnuts or 1 cup nut meal from nut milk (see page 120)

½ cup sugar

1 teaspoon ground cinnamon

½ teaspoon salt

Flour for dusting

½ cup unsalted butter, melted

1. Put the milk in a small saucepan. Heat the milk over medium heat until tiny bubbles begin to form around the edge of pan, but do not let the milk boil. Remove the milk from the heat. Add the butter and the ⅓ cup sugar and stir until the butter has melted and the sugar has dissolved. Pour the mixture into a large bowl and let cool until it is slightly above room temperature, 5 to 10 minutes.

2. In a small bowl, combine the yeast and the pinch of sugar. Add the warm water and stir to dissolve. Let stand for 5 minutes, then pour into the butter mixture. Combine 4 cups of the flour with the salt in another bowl. Stir the flour mixture into the yeast mixture and beat until smooth. Cover with a kitchen towel and let rise in a warm place until doubled in size, about 2 hours.

3. After the dough has risen, stir in the remaining ¼ cup flour. Use your hands to knead the dough in the bowl for 4 to 5 minutes. It should be soft and springy but not sticky.

4. Preheat the oven to 350°F. Grease a 10-inch Bundt pan.

5. To make the topping: Put the nuts, sugar, cinnamon, and salt in a food processor and pulse until the mixture is the texture of coarse meal, about 30 seconds. If you are using nut meal from making nut milk, mix the ingredients in a bowl.

6. Dust a worksurface well with flour. Using well-floured hands, pinch off small pieces of the dough and roll them into 1-inch balls. Take each ball and roll it into the butter, then into the cinnamon mixture, arranging the balls in a ring in the pan as you go. Repeat to make another layer of dough balls. Top with the remaining butter and topping.

7. Bake until the bread is golden brown and a toothpick inserted into the center comes out relatively clean, 45 to 55 minutes. Let cool in the pan for 5 to 10 minutes. Run a blunt knife along edges of bread to free it from the pan. Invert the pan onto a serving dish and unmold the bread.

Mixed Nut, Maple, and Dried Cranberry Granola

This nutty granola makes a protein-packed way to start the day and has less sugar than most commercial varieties. You can substitute your favorite nuts and dried fruits to create your own signature recipe. Kids can bring the granola along to share on sleepovers or wrap it attractively to present as gifts. [MAKES ABOUT 4 CUPS]

Cooking spray or canola oil for pan

2 cups old-fashioned rolled oats

⅓ cup chopped walnuts

⅓ cup chopped almonds

2 tablespoons firmly packed light brown sugar

⅓ cup dried cranberries

¼ teaspoon salt

¼ cup maple syrup

3 tablespoons canola oil

1 teaspoon freshly grated lemon zest

1. Preheat the oven to 275°F. Grease a rimmed baking sheet with cooking spray or oil.

2. In a large bowl, toss together the oats, walnuts, almonds, brown sugar, cranberries, and salt.

3. In a small saucepan, combine the maple syrup, canola oil, lemon zest, and 1 tablespoon water. Bring the maple mixture to a simmer. Drizzle the warm maple mixture over the oat mixture. Use your hands to work the liquid and dry mixtures together. Scrape onto the baking sheet and make teaspoon-size clusters. The clusters can be loose and touching.

4. Bake the granola for 30 minutes. Do not stir the granola, so that the clusters stay intact. Let cool completely. Store the granola in an airtight container in cool, dark place for up to 3 months.

KIDS CAN
grease the baking sheet • measure and toss the raw ingredients • coat the ingredients with the maple mixture

Almond Milk

Nut milk, an increasingly popular substitute for cow's milk, is delicious and easy to make. When you produce your own nut milk, you can use less sugar than is found in most commercially available products. Homemade nut milk is also less expensive. Almonds are one of the best nuts for milk. You can also use hazelnuts, but peanuts and walnuts are not recommended because they have a bitter, oily flavor.

After squeezing the milk from the nuts, you'll be left with nut meal, which you can use to make cookies. If you can't use the meal right away, you can freeze it in lock-top freezer bags for up to 2 months. [MAKES 3 CUPS]

1 cup almonds

3 cups water

1 to 2 tablespoons honey

1 teaspoon pure vanilla extract

⅛ teaspoon salt

KIDS CAN
measure the ingredients and put them in the blender • pulse the blender • strain the liquefied nuts

1. Put the almonds in a small bowl. Add water to cover by 2 inches. Refrigerate overnight.

2. Drain the almonds and place in a blender. Add the water, honey, vanilla, and salt. Pulse in bursts of 5 to 10 seconds until the almonds are liquefied, about 30 seconds total.

3. Place a double layer of cheesecloth in a colander or strainer with a handle and set over a bowl. Slowly pour the nut mixture over the cheesecloth, keeping the mixture in the center. Pick up the corners of the cheesecloth, then lift and twist the cheesecloth to press out the milk. Keep twisting until all the milk is in the bowl.

4. Pour the milk into bottles or a pitcher. The milk will keep for up to 3 days in the refrigerator. Reserve the nut meal for making cookies (see page 115).

Winter Squashes

Although winter squashes are harvested in autumn, they are so named because they last through the winter. Unlike tender summer squashes, which are harvested young, these hard squashes are picked when fully mature. With their thick skins and colors of red, white, orange, and even blue, they are beautiful to look at and display in the kitchen. The best-known winter squash is the pumpkin, the mascot for fall. These versatile vegetables are wonderful in both sweet and savory dishes, from soups to breads and cookies. The roasted seeds make delicious snacks.

Choosing: Select a squash or pumpkin that has hard skin and no sign of bruises. Sometimes you will see a squash with a flat side, indicating where it lay on the ground while growing.

Storing: Squashes and pumpkins will last for up to 2 months stored in a cool, dry, dark place with good ventilation.

Varieties: squashes: acorn, butternut, delicata, hubbard, spaghetti, turban; pumpkins: Cinderella, Sugar Pie

Roasted Spaghetti Squash with Butter and Cheese

The stringy flesh of spaghetti squash looks and tastes like spaghetti, especially when roasted and garnished with Parmesan cheese. You can also top the strands of spaghetti squash with homemade tomato sauce (page 87). [SERVES 6 TO 8]

1 medium spaghetti squash, about 3 pounds

3 tablespoons olive oil

1 teaspoon coarse sea salt

2 tablespoons salted butter

2 tablespoons finely chopped flat-leaf parsley

¼ cup grated Parmesan cheese

1. Preheat the oven to 375°F.

2. Cut the spaghetti squash in half lengthwise. Place the halves, cut-side up, on a baking sheet. Drizzle the olive oil evenly over the squash. Sprinkle each half with ½ teaspoon of the salt. Roast until the squash is tender, about 1½ hours. Let stand until the squash halves are cool enough to handle.

3. Use a large spoon to scoop up the cooked squash, working across each half rather than lengthwise. The flesh should separate into strands. Put the strands in a large bowl. Add the butter and parsley and toss until the butter has melted. Sprinkle with the cheese before serving.

KIDS CAN
drizzle olive oil and sprinkle salt on squash halves • scoop out cooked squash and separate it into strands • grate cheese • toss squash with the butter and parsley

Roasted Pumpkin Seeds

Pumpkins are native to Central America, and the toasted, spiced seeds are a popular snack in Mexico. When you and your kids carve a pumpkin, be sure to save the seeds for roasting. The small, tender seeds from delicata, butternut, and acorn squashes can also be roasted. This recipe calls for an optional touch of spicy cayenne, but feel free to leave out altogether or substitute another spice such as cumin, turmeric, or dried oregano. [MAKES ABOUT 1 CUP]

1 medium pumpkin, about 5 pounds

⅛ teaspoon cayenne pepper (optional)

¼ teaspoon paprika

½ teaspoon coarse sea salt

1 teaspoon olive oil

1. Preheat the oven to 250°F.

2. Cut the top off the pumpkin. Using your hands, scoop out the seeds. Put the seeds in a colander and rinse to remove any bits of pumpkin flesh. Spread the seeds on a kitchen towel and pat dry.

3. In a small bowl, stir together the cayenne, paprika, salt, and olive oil. Add the seeds. Use a spoon to stir the seeds until they are coated evenly with the spice mixture.

4. Spread the seeds in a single layer on a baking sheet. Roast until the seeds are golden brown and crisp, about 30 minutes. Let cool. Store the seeds in an airtight container for up to 3 months.

KIDS CAN
scoop out the pumpkin seeds • mix the seeds with the spices • spread the coated seeds on the baking sheet

Pumpkin Tartlets with Crispy Sugar Crust

Early settlers in America sliced off the tops of pumpkins, removed the seeds, filled the insides with milk, spices, and honey, and then baked the pumpkins in hot ashes. This was the origin of pumpkin pie. Instead of making a pumpkin pie for the holidays, you can try these tartlets, which are elegant single-serving desserts. The topping adds a sweet and crunchy texture. If you like, you can omit it and serve the tartlets with dollops of whipped cream.

You will need a standard 12-cup muffin pan or 12 mini tartlet pans (3 inches in diameter). You will want to have on hand a flattened paper muffin-cup liner to use as a template for cutting out dough rounds. [MAKES 12 TARTLETS]

FOR THE FILLING

2 cups Homemade Pumpkin Purée (page 129)

⅔ cup firmly packed dark brown sugar

1 teaspoon ground cinnamon

½ teaspoon ground cloves

½ teaspoon ground nutmeg

1 teaspoon pure vanilla extract

½ teaspoon salt

2 eggs, lightly beaten

1 cup heavy cream

½ cup milk

1. To make the filling: In a medium bowl, combine the pumpkin purée, brown sugar, cinnamon, cloves, nutmeg, vanilla, salt, eggs, cream, and milk. Stir with a whisk until combined.

2. To make the topping: In a small bowl, stir together the brown sugar, melted butter, and chopped nuts.

3. Preheat the oven to 400°F.

4. On a lightly floured work surface, roll out the Flaky Pastry Dough to a generous ⅛ inch thick. Using a flattened cupcake liner as a guide, cut out 12 circles. Gently press the circles into 12 muffin cups or 12 mini tartlet pans. Loosely crimp the edges, letting them hang over the pans by ¼ inch. If using tartlet pans, place them on a baking sheet.

continued

FOR THE TOPPING

¼ cup loosely packed dark brown
  sugar

3 tablespoons unsalted butter,
  melted

½ cup chopped walnuts or pecans

Flaky Pastry Dough (page 79)

5. Ladle the filling into the lined muffin cups or tartlet pans, filling each to within ¼ inch of the rim. Bake for 10 minutes. Remove from the oven and sprinkle 1 to 2 teaspoons of the topping over each tartlet. Reduce the oven temperature to 350°F and bake until the filling is puffed and the crusts are golden, about 25 minutes. A toothpick inserted into the center will come out clean. Let cool before serving.

KIDS CAN
measure ingredients for
and help make the dough •
measure and mix filling
and topping ingredients •
fill muffin cups or
tartlet pans

Homemade Pumpkin Purée

Many people buy pumpkin purée in a can for making pies and other recipes, but it is easy to prepare at home with kids. The best variety to use is Sugar Pie, which has a light-orange flesh and sweet flavor. A 6-pound pumpkin will make enough purée for 12 tartlets (page 127). [MAKES 2 CUPS]

1 Sugar Pie pumpkin, about
  6 pounds

4 cups water

1. Preheat the oven to 350°F.

2. Cut the pumpkin in half lengthwise. Place each half, cut-side down, in a shallow baking dish. Add 2 cups water to each dish. Bake until the flesh is very soft, 2 hours. Test the halves by inserting a sharp knife through the skin. If there is no resistance, the pumpkin is thoroughly cooked.

3. Remove the halves from the oven and scoop out the seeds. Set the seeds aside to roast (see page 124). Let the pumpkin halves stand until they are cool enough to handle.

4. Use a large serving spoon to scoop out the flesh. Put the flesh in a food processor and process until smooth, 3 to 4 minutes. Line a colander or fine-mesh sieve with cheesecloth and place over a bowl. Pour in the purée and let drain for about 1½ hours. It is important to drain as much water as possible from the purée before using it as a filling. Discard the liquid in the bowl. Cover and refrigerate for up to 2 days.

KIDS CAN
scoop out the flesh from the cooked pumpkin halves • help purée the flesh in the food processor

WINTER

Although many people think of the winter as the time when most fields lie fallow, many farmers' markets still have varieties of potatoes, winter greens, and citrus fruits. This is the season for making comforting casseroles like cauliflower with ham and Cheddar cheese sauce and tasty side dishes like onion rings and mashed sweet potatoes. Preparing sauerkraut is a fun project for kids. They can also help cook festive holiday treats including candied citrus peel and lemon curd bars, as well as decorate wreaths with colorful seasonal fruit.

Cabbages

With its crunchy texture and robust flavor, cabbage makes up for what it lacks in glamour with longevity and versatility. Cabbage varieties have a wide array of shapes: oval, drumhead (flattened ball), pointed, and round, with leaves varying from smooth and waxy to crinkled. You'll see many colors: rich shades of purple and red, dark green, bluish gray, and the palest celadon.

Choosing: Look for firm heads with unblemished leaves. The core should not appear dried. Cabbages that have a dry core or leaves that are beginning to unfurl are past their prime.

Storage: Cabbage wilts, so make sure to store it, unrinsed, in a plastic bag in the refrigerator, where it will keep for up to 3 weeks.

Varieties: Early Jersey Wakefield, Grenadier, napa, Ruby Ball, savoy

Traditional German Sauerkraut

Sauerkraut is fermented cabbage, and the process of making sauerkraut from scratch is a practice in patience, as it can take up to a month. Sliced cabbage is layered with salt and packed tightly into a crock or other ceramic vessel. The fermenting process yields lactic acid, the substance that makes sauerkraut sour. You and your kids can look on this as more of a science project than a recipe. Be forewarned: The fermenting cabbage smells like stinky socks! However, when the sauerkraut is rinsed and cooked, it is delicious.

The traditional cabbage for sauerkraut is green cabbage. For this recipe, the cabbage is fermented in a big ceramic crock or plastic bucket. You will also need a dinner-size plate that will fit inside your chosen container. [MAKES ABOUT 2 QUARTS]

1 head green cabbage, about
  5 pounds

3 tablespoons coarse sea salt
  or pickling salt

KIDS CAN
layer the cabbage and salt • pound and help weight the cabbage • check the fermenting cabbage and skim any foam • help rinse and drain the finished sauerkraut

1. Cut the cabbage in half and remove the core. Cut the cabbage crosswise into strips about ¼ inch wide. Layer the cabbage strips and salt in a ceramic crock or plastic bucket. Pound with a mortar or wooden spoon until a thin layer of juice covers the cabbage. More liquid will appear as the salt draws moisture from the cabbage. Put a plate on top of the cabbage. Weight the plate with 10 to 15 pounds of clean bricks or rocks. The weights will push the juices from the cabbage. Cover the crock or bucket with a pillowcase to keep out dust.

2. Place the crock in a location where the temperature is between 60°F and 75°F. The cooler the temperature, the longer the fermentation will take. Check the cabbage daily and skim off the foam as it appears. Rinse the plate and replace it and the weights on top of the cabbage.

3. When the fermentation is complete, no more bubbles will appear, and the cabbage will have been transformed into raw sauerkraut. This will take 2 to 4 weeks. Store the sauerkraut in its liquid in the refrigerator for up to 1 month. Drain and rinse the sauerkraut when you are ready to cook it.

Classic Coleslaw

Creamy and crunchy, homemade coleslaw is an easy make-ahead dish. You have several choices of methods for shredding the cabbage. A box grater is the best tool for kids of all ages. Older kids can use a mandoline, with your help. A food processor not only is fast but also delivers the finest pieces. For the most rustic shred, you can cut the cabbage with a sharp knife. For cutting the cabbage by hand, remove the core and cut the head crosswise into ¼-inch-wide strips. You can experiment to find the best method for your kids.

[SERVES 6 TO 8]

1 head cabbage, cored and shredded

1 carrot, coarsely grated

2 teaspoons sugar

½ teaspoon coarse sea salt

⅛ teaspoon ground pepper

¼ cup milk

½ cup mayonnaise

3 tablespoons buttermilk

1 tablespoon distilled white vinegar

2 tablespoons freshly squeezed lemon juice

1. Place the cabbage in a large bowl and add the carrot.

2. In a small bowl, combine the sugar, salt, pepper, milk, mayonnaise, buttermilk, vinegar, and lemon juice. Whisk to mix well.

3. Pour the mixture over the cabbage and carrot. Toss to coat the vegetables evenly. Cover and refrigerate for at least 2 hours before serving.

KIDS CAN
shred the cabbage •
grate the carrot •
measure the ingredients
for and mix the dressing •
toss the vegetables
with the dressing

Chinese Chicken Salad with Napa Cabbage

Napa cabbage, with its delicate texture and flavor, has more in common with heads of lettuce than with traditional large, dense cabbages. The leaves are tender and pair well with the tangy-sweet flavors of this Chinese-inspired dressing. The cabbage retains its appealing texture when marinated, so you can make this salad a day ahead and let it sit to absorb the seasonings. This is a handy dish to prepare with leftover or store-bought roast chicken. [SERVES 4]

1 skinless, boneless chicken breast half

1 teaspoon salt

2 bay leaves

1 medium head napa cabbage, 2½ to 3 pounds

3 scallions, including green tops, finely chopped

FOR THE DRESSING

3 teaspoons soy sauce

1 teaspoon Asian sesame oil

2 tablespoons peanut oil

2 tablespoons rice vinegar

1 teaspoon sugar

1 teaspoon freshly squeezed lime juice

1. Place the chicken breast in a small saucepan and add water to cover. Bring to a boil and add the salt and bay leaves. Reduce the heat to medium and cook until the chicken is opaque throughout, about 20 minutes. Remove the chicken from the pan and let stand until it is cool enough to handle. Using your fingers, pull the chicken meat apart, shredding it into pieces about ¼ inch thick and 1 inch long.

2. Trim the stem end of the cabbage and remove the core. Cut the cabbage crosswise into ¼-inch-wide strips. Rinse the strips and pat dry. Place the strips in a large bowl. Add the scallions and chicken and toss to combine.

3. To make the dressing: In a small bowl, combine the soy sauce, sesame oil, peanut oil, rice vinegar, sugar, and lime juice. Whisk to blend.

4. Pour the dressing over the salad and toss. You can serve the salad immediately or refrigerate it for up to 24 hours and serve chilled.

KIDS CAN
shred the cooked chicken • rinse and dry the cabbage • toss the cabbage and chicken • measure the ingredients for and mix the dressing • toss the salad with the dressing

Broccoli, Cauliflower, and Brussels Sprouts

Broccoli, cauliflower, and Brussels sprouts are all descendants of early, wild cabbages. But unlike cabbages, they grow on thick, fleshy stalks. Kids may find the flavors of this trio too strong and bitter, but the recipes here have been developed to appeal to kids' palates. Cauliflower, in particular, comes in a variety of shapes and colors, including the pyramidal Romanesco and the aptly named, brilliant orange Cheddar variety. In most cases, broccoli can be substituted for cauliflower.

Choosing: Broccoli, Brussels sprouts, and cauliflower should all have tight florets or heads. Avoid broccoli with florets that have started to open to tiny yellow flowers. The leaves of Brussels sprouts should not be yellow, and those on heads of cauliflower should be free of brown or soft spots. Cauliflower bruises easily and needs to be handled with care.

Storage: All three vegetables will keep well in plastic bags in the refrigerator for up to 1 week.

Varieties: broccoli: Green Goliath, Packman; Brussels sprouts: Long Island, Royal Marvel; cauliflower: Romanesco, Cheddar, Igloo, Snowball, Violetta

Stir-Fried Broccoli with Chicken

Broccoli is one of many vegetables that is most flavorful when eaten raw or just cooked through. It's a green vegetable that kids like as long as it is not overcooked. This fast and fresh recipe makes a great weekday family meal that kids can help put on the table.
[SERVES 6]

1 cup brown or white rice

1 head broccoli (about 1 pound)

¼ cup canola oil

1 skinless, boneless whole chicken breast, cut into ½-inch cubes

2 cloves garlic, sliced

1 teaspoon grated fresh ginger

2 tablespoons soy sauce

1 teaspoon Asian sesame oil

1. Cook the rice according to the package instructions.

2. Remove the stems from the broccoli. Separate the broccoli into bite-size florets. Peel and cut the stems into coin-size pieces.

3. Place a large skillet over high heat, add the canola oil, and heat until almost smoking. Add the chicken and garlic and cook, stirring constantly, until browned, about 3 minutes. Add the broccoli and ginger. Cook, stirring, until the ginger is fragrant and the broccoli is starting to brown, about 3 minutes. Add the soy sauce and sesame oil. Toss to coat the vegetables and chicken and remove the pan from the heat. Serve immediately with the rice.

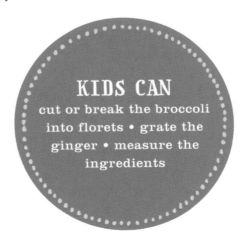

KIDS CAN
cut or break the broccoli into florets • grate the ginger • measure the ingredients

Cauliflower, Ham, and Cheddar Cheese Bake

This recipe transforms cauliflower into a version of macaroni and cheese that even the pickiest eater will love. Kids can use their hands to break the florets from the head. Any type of cauliflower will work for this recipe, and for fun we love using a yellow variety called Cheddar. You can also use broccoli. [SERVES 6]

1 tablespoon olive oil

2 cloves garlic, crushed

1 head yellow or white cauliflower, about ½ pound

1 cup cubed, cooked ham

FOR THE CHEESE SAUCE

3 tablespoons unsalted butter

2 tablespoons all-purpose flour

1 cup milk

¼ teaspoon salt

½ cup grated mild white or yellow Cheddar cheese

¼ cup bread crumbs

1. Preheat the oven to 400°F. Coat the bottom and sides of a 6-cup baking dish with the olive oil. Then rub the bottom and sides with the crushed garlic. Discard the garlic cloves.

2. Separate the cauliflower into bite-size florets. Place the florets and the ham in the dish and toss to combine.

3. To make the cheese sauce: In a small saucepan over low heat, melt the butter. Add the flour and stir until the flour and butter just form a paste. Whisk in ¼ cup of the milk and stir until the mixture begins to thicken, about 3 minutes. Stirring constantly, add the remaining ¾ cup milk a little at a time. Add the salt and continue to cook, stirring, until the sauce is thick and clings to the spoon. Add the cheese and stir until it is melted and fully incorporated.

4. Pour the sauce evenly over the ham and cauliflower. Sprinkle with the bread crumbs.

5. Bake until the cauliflower is tender and the cheese sauce is bubbling and starting to brown, 25 to 30 minutes. Serve immediately.

KIDS CAN
separate the cauliflower florets • oil the baking dish and rub with the garlic • grate the cheese • measure ingredients • help stir the sauce

Brussels Sprouts with Bacon and Toasted Walnuts

At farmers' markets, Brussels sprouts are often sold on their big stalks. When kids see this, they might be encouraged to give these miniature cabbages another chance. Their small size makes them fun to peel. In this recipe, any bitterness is offset by bacon—and bacon makes everything taste better. [SERVES 4]

1 pound Brussels sprouts

4 slices bacon, cut crosswise into
    ½-inch pieces

1 tablespoon olive oil

¼ cup chopped walnuts, toasted

¼ teaspoon salt

1. Pull the bottom leaves off the Brussels sprouts. Trim the ends. Cut the sprouts in half lengthwise.

2. Heat a skillet over a medium heat and add the bacon. Cook the bacon, turning often, until crisp, about 5 minutes. Transfer the cooked bacon to a plate covered with a paper towel.

3. Drain any excess bacon fat from the skillet, return it to medium heat, and warm the olive oil. Add the Brussels sprouts and cook, stirring often, until they turn bright green and start to brown, about 7 minutes. Add the nuts, salt, and bacon. Continue to cook, stirring occasionally, to blend the flavors, 3 to 4 minutes. Serve immediately.

KIDS CAN
pull the bottom leaves
from the sprouts and trim
the ends • measure the
ingredients

Citrus Fruits

At a time when the offerings in the market seem limited, lemons, limes, oranges, and other citrus fruits provide a vibrant splash of color and flavor. If you live in or near a citrus-growing climate, you might also discover mandarins, tangerines, grapefruits, and kumquats to brighten up your menus. A bowl of citrus fruits makes a pretty winter centerpiece.

Choosing: Ripe citrus should feel heavy, a sign of high juice content. Ask the vendor to confirm the proper coloring that indicates ripeness for the fruit you choose.

Storing: Most citrus fruits will keep for up to 3 weeks on the kitchen counter in a bowl. Some varieties will have a shorter shelf life.

Varieties: grapefruits: Marsh, Ruby Red; lemons: Eureka, Lisbon, Meyer; limes: Kaffir, Key; oranges: blood, Cara Cara, navel, Seville; other: Clementine, kumquat, pomelo, rangpur, satsuma Mandarin, tangelo, tangerine

Mix-and-Match Citrus Curd

Many kids like sour flavors, and this rich curd, at once sweet and tangy, can be slathered on toast, baked into bars or a tart, or eaten right from the jar. Lemon is the most popular flavor for curd; however, this recipe is versatile, so you can use the citrus fruit of your choice, whether lemon, lime, tangelo, or blood orange for a vividly colored curd.

[MAKES 3 HALF-PINT JARS]

3 egg yolks

⅓ cup sugar

Grated zest from 1 citrus fruit

½ cup strained, freshly squeezed citrus juice

6 tablespoons unsalted butter, cut into pieces

KIDS CAN
crack the eggs • grate the zest • juice the fruit • cut up the butter • stir and strain the curd

1. Thoroughly wash three half-pint canning jars and their lids and screw bands. Put the jars, lids, and screw bands in a large pot and add water to cover. Bring to a boil and continue to boil for 15 minutes to sterilize the jars, lids, and bands. Turn off the heat and leave the jars in the hot water until ready to use.

2. In a medium nonreactive saucepan, combine the egg yolks, sugar, and zest. Whisk the mixture until it is pale yellow. Warm the mixture over medium heat, stirring constantly. Add the juice and butter, and continue to whisk while the butter melts. It is important to whisk constantly so that the eggs do not cook and form lumps and the mixture does not scorch. When the mixture has thickened and clings to the back of a spoon, remove it from the heat.

3. Place a fine-mesh sieve over a small bowl. Use a rubber spatula to scrape the curd into the sieve. Strain the curd to remove any solids and ensure a smooth and creamy texture.

4. Using tongs, lift the jars, lids, and screw bands from the hot water and dry thoroughly. Ladle the curd into the jars. Wipe each jar rim clean with a damp towel, then top with a lid and seal tightly with a screw band. Let the jars cool. Store the curd in the refrigerator for up to 1 week.

Buttery Citrus Curd Bars

Once you've made citrus curd, it is a snap to prepare these buttery bars. The work will go fast—and be more fun—if kids help press the dough into the pan while you make the curd. You can bake the bars in a rectangular pan or, for a more decorative look, a 9-inch fluted tart pan with a removable bottom. If using a tart pan, cut wedges rather than bars.

[MAKES 12 BARS]

2 cups sifted all-purpose flour

1 cup confectioners' sugar, plus ¼ cup for dusting

1 cup unsalted butter, melted

1½ cups Mix-and-Match Citrus Curd (page 143)

1. Preheat the oven to 350°F. Grease a 9-by-13-inch baking pan.

2. In a medium bowl, stir together the flour and the 1 cup confectioners' sugar. Using your fingers, work the melted butter into the dry ingredients until the mixture is moist and crumbly. Place the dough in the baking pan. Press it evenly into the bottom and ½ inch up the sides of the pan.

3. Bake until the crust is just golden brown, about 15 minutes. Remove the pan from the oven and let cool for 10 minutes. Spread the curd over the crust. Return the pan to the oven and bake until the curd is lightly golden, about 10 minutes. Let cool completely. Cut into bars and dust with the ¼ cup confectioners' sugar before serving.

KIDS CAN

grease the pan • sift the flour • measure and mix the ingredients for the dough • press the dough into the pan • cut the bars and dust them with sugar

Candied Citrus Curls

Candied citrus is a beautiful holiday confection for topping cakes, embellishing iced cookies, or giving as gifts. It is made by boiling the zest, the outermost layer of the peel, in a sugar syrup. The most commonly purchased candied citrus is made from lemons and oranges, but the pomelo has fragrant, thick zest that is perfect for candying. Little hands can wrap the strips of zest around a chopstick to make a cute corkscrew shape. [MAKES 1 CUP]

2 lemons or oranges, or 1 small
 grapefruit or pomelo

1½ cups granulated sugar

1½ cups water

KIDS CAN
cut out parchment
paper • measure the
ingredients • roll the
candied strips in sugar
and twist them into
corkscrew
shapes

1. Line a baking sheet with parchment paper.

2. Use a sharp vegetable peeler to cut long strips of zest from the citrus, making sure to avoid including too much of the bitter white pith. The longer the strips, the easier it is to make curls. Trim each strip lengthwise to about ¼ inch wide.

3. In a small saucepan, combine 1¼ cups of the sugar and the water. Bring to a boil and stir constantly until the sugar completely dissolves. Stir in the zest strips and cook until translucent, 10 to 15 minutes. Drain the strips.

4. Lay the zest strips on the baking sheet. Sprinkle the strips with the remaining ¼ cup sugar and roll in the sugar to coat them completely. Twist each strip around a chopstick or a straw to create a corkscrew shape. Arrange the curls on the baking sheet and let dry overnight. As the strips harden, they will keep their curled shape. Store in an airtight container for up to 6 months.

Holiday Wreath

Unadorned wreaths with fresh greenery are often available at farmers' markets. Kids can help decorate them with fresh citrus fruits in a variety of sizes and bright colors.

[MAKES 1 WREATH]

Wire snips

24-gauge wire

6 small oranges

3 small lemons or limes

8 kumquats

1 purchased wreath

1 yard of 3- to 4-inch-wide ribbon

Scissors

KIDS CAN
skewer the fruit •
help attach them to the
wreath • tie and trim
the bow

1. Using wire snips, cut a 12-inch length of wire for each fruit. Skewer each fruit through the center, working up from one end. Fold the wire over and twist to secure the wire around the fruit.

2. Beginning in the center of the bottom of the wreath, attach clusters of fruit. You can work up both sides of the wreath, or you can work up one side for an asymmetrical design. Secure each fruit by wrapping the wires around the wreath and securing them at the back, twisting them tightly. Snip off any excess wire and tuck the ends into the greenery.

3. Loop the ribbon through the top center of the wreath and tie a big bow. Trim the ends of the ribbon at an angle.

4. If kept in a cool place—a front door in winter, for example—the fruit should slowly dry out and keep for 2 to 3 weeks. In warm climates, the wreath will last 4 to 7 days.

Onions

There are two basic types of onions: those that make you cry (often called hot onions) and those that don't (known as sweet onions). Hot onions, such as Giant Red Hamburger and Yellow Ebenezer, sting when you bite into them and make you cry when you cut them because they contain strong sulfur compounds. Sweet onions, such as Walla Walla and Vidalia, have much less bite and don't make you tear up. If you want to hold back the tears, ask the vendor at the market to guide you to the sweet onions.

Choosing: Onions should be firm and free of bruises, soft spots, and sprouts. They should have thin, papery skins.

Storing: Onions are best stored in a cool, dry place with relatively low humidity, rather than in the refrigerator. They will keep for up to 1 month. If an onion sprouts, cut away the sprouts and use the onion immediately.

Varieties: Bermuda, Giant Red Hamburger, Italian (cipollini), Red Holland, Snow White Hybrid, Spanish, Vidalia, Walla Walla, Yellow Ebenezer

Baked Cornmeal Onion Rings

These crispy rings will warm up any winter evening. They are baked, rather than deep-fried, and are fun for kids to make. Sweet onions are preferred for a tears-free experience. Larger onions are easier to work with. Dipping the onions in the batter is a bit messy, so set up your workspace with a tablecloth or other covering that is easy to clean.

[SERVES 4 TO 6]

2 large yellow onions, peeled and cut crosswise into ½-inch-thick slices

2 cups buttermilk

1 teaspoon salt

½ teaspoon pepper

1½ cups all-purpose flour

½ cup yellow cornmeal

4 tablespoons canola oil

KIDS CAN
separate the onion slices into rings • measure and mix ingredients for the batter • dip onions in batter and cornmeal mixture

1. Preheat the oven to 375°F.

2. Separate the onion slices into rings. In a large bowl, stir together the buttermilk, ½ teaspoon of the salt, and ¼ teaspoon of the pepper. Immerse the onion rings in the buttermilk mixture.

3. In another large bowl, combine the flour, cornmeal, remaining ½ teaspoon salt, and remaining ¼ teaspoon pepper. Pour the cornmeal mixture onto a large platter.

4. Coat two baking sheets with the canola oil, using 2 tablespoons for each. Place the sheets in the oven and heat for 5 to 7 minutes. The heated oil will help give the onion rings a crispy texture.

5. With tongs or fingers, remove the onion rings from the buttermilk mixture and put them in the cornmeal mixture. Turn the rings in the cornmeal mixture to coat them evenly. Remove the baking sheets from the oven and arrange the rings on the heated sheets in a single layer. Bake until the undersides of the rings have started to brown, about 10 minutes. Remove the sheets from the oven and turn over the rings. Return to the oven and bake for another 5 minutes or until the bottoms are browned. Serve hot.

Potatoes

Although potatoes are often called root vegetables, they are classified as tubers, underground stems that carry the nutrients for growing new plants. Most people know the large russet potato, ideal for baking, mashing, and frying. Many others, including Yukon gold, White Rose, and fingerling, are just as versatile in the kitchen.

Choosing: Select potatoes that are firm and free of wrinkles, bruises, sprouts, or buds. Black spots or greenish patches indicate that the tubers have been exposed to light and improperly stored. If you are cooking whole potatoes all at once, choose potatoes of uniform size.

Storage: Potatoes are best stored in a cool, dark place, not in the refrigerator. They will keep for up to 1 month.

Varieties: fingerling, Irish Cobbler, purple, Red Pontiac, russet, Sangre, White Rose, Yellow Finn, Yukon gold

Shepherd's Pie with Best Mashed Potatoes

Like the tamale pie (page 64), this recipe is two dishes in one. It combines two beloved winter comfort foods kids love: mashed potatoes and meat loaf. [SERVES 6 TO 8]

2 pounds russet, Yukon gold, or fingerling potatoes, peeled and cut into chunks

½ cup milk

4 tablespoons unsalted butter

3 teaspoons salt

1 teaspoon ground pepper

2 tablespoons olive oil

½ medium sweet onion, chopped

2 medium carrots, finely chopped

2 ribs celery, finely chopped

1 pound ground lamb or beef

1 teaspoon chopped thyme

2 tablespoons tomato paste

1. Put the potato chunks in a pot, add water to cover, and bring to a boil. Cook until the potatoes are tender and fall apart when pierced with a fork, 8 to 10 minutes. Drain the potatoes, return them to the pot, and let cool. Add the milk and butter and mash with a potato masher or back of a wooden spoon until creamy. Stir in 1 teaspoon of the salt and ½ teaspoon of the pepper.

2. Preheat the oven to 400°F. Have ready a 2-quart baking dish.

3. In a large skillet over medium heat, warm the olive oil. Add the onion, carrots, and celery and cook until the vegetables are softened, about 5 minutes. Add the ground meat and cook, stirring to break up any clumps, until the meat is no longer pink, 4 minutes. Add the thyme, tomato paste, remaining 2 teaspoons salt, and remaining ½ teaspoon pepper, and stir to combine. Cook until the mixture thickens, about 4 minutes.

4. Spoon the meat mixture into the baking dish and spread in an even layer. Spread the mashed potatoes evenly over the top. Bake until the top is golden, about 30 minutes. Serve hot.

KIDS CAN
peel the potatoes • mash the cooked potatoes • measure the ingredients • top the meat mixture with the mashed potatoes

Gnocchi with Parmesan Cheese

For kids, mashing the potatoes and rolling the dough is as fun as eating these savory Italian dumplings. Yukon gold potatoes lend a delicate and mild flavor to the dish. This recipe comes from an Italian friend who says that the key to success is knowing when to stop adding the flour to the dumpling mixture. You can serve the gnocchi with melted butter and grated Parmesan cheese, as here, or with homemade tomato sauce (see page 87).

If you prefer to bake the potatoes, which works well when using russets, cook them in a preheated 350°F oven until tender, about 45 minutes. Cut the hot potatoes in half, scoop out the flesh, and pass through a ricer into a large bowl. [SERVES 6]

6 medium Yukon gold or
    russet potatoes

⅓ cup semolina flour

2 cups all-purpose flour, plus more
    for work surface

1 egg, plus 1 egg yolk

4 tablespoons extra-virgin olive oil

1 teaspoon salt

½ cup finely grated Parmesan
    cheese

1. Place the potatoes in a large pot and add cold water to cover. Bring to a boil and cook the potatoes until they can easily be pierced all the way through with a sharp knife, about 40 minutes. Drain the potatoes and let them stand until they are cool enough to handle. Peel the potatoes. Pass them through a ricer into a bowl, or put them in a bowl and mash with a wooden spoon.

2. Sprinkle a large baking dish with the semolina flour. This will keep the gnocchi from sticking before you are ready to cook them.

3. Pour 3 quarts water into the same pot and bring to a boil.

4. Dust a work surface with all-purpose flour and mound the mashed potatoes into a mountain shape. Make a depression in the peak of the mountain, crack the egg into the depression, and add the egg yolk. Using your hands, mix the eggs into the mashed potatoes. Add 2 tablespoons of the olive oil and the salt, and begin adding the 2 cups all-purpose flour, about ½ cup at a time, mixing with your hands to form a smooth dough that doesn't stick. The dough will take as much flour as you add, but too much can make the gnocchi tough.

5. Break off a baseball-size round of dough. Roll it on the floured work surface into a rope about ¾ inch thick. Cut the rope into 1-inch pieces and place the pieces in the semolina-lined baking dish. Continue to roll the dough and cut pieces.

6. Working in batches, slip the gnocchi into the boiling water and cook until they float to the top, 2 to 3 minutes. Use a slotted spoon to remove them from the boiling water and place them in a serving dish. Add the remaining 2 tablespoons olive oil and toss gently to coat the gnocchi. Sprinkle with the Parmesan before serving.

Sweet Potatoes

Sweet potatoes are large, starchy oblong-shaped tubers that are a native to South America. At farmers' markets, you may see sweet potatoes in a range of colors: with dark rust or creamy white skins and with orange-red, yellow, or tan flesh. Though commonly used in side dishes, sweet potatoes make a sumptuous substitution for pumpkin in pies or cookies. If a sweet potato in your kitchen starts to sprout, partially submerge it in a shallow dish or jar of water, place in a sunny spot, and wait for a beautiful purple vine to take off.

Choosing: Sweet potatoes should be firm with evenly colored, unblemished skins.

Storing: Keep sweet potatoes in a cool, dry, dark place. They can be stored for up to 2 weeks.

Varieties: Amish Red, Carolina Ruby, Edna Evans, Garnet

Candied Mashed Sweet Potatoes with Pecans

Mashed potatoes are already a kid favorite. Imagine their smiles when they discover the sweet side of potatoes. This recipe can be made with any available variety of sweet potatoes. Serve this warm, creamy side dish for breakfast or with Thanksgiving dinner.
[SERVES 6]

2 pounds sweet potatoes, peeled and cut into 1-inch chunks

4 tablespoons salted butter

¼ teaspoon salt

⅓ cup milk

⅓ cup firmly packed dark brown sugar

½ cup coarsely chopped pecans, toasted

KIDS CAN
help cut the potatoes into chunks • mash the potatoes • measure the ingredients • mix the ingredients with the mashed potatoes

1. Preheat the oven to 350°F.

2. Bring a large pot of water to a boil. Slip the sweet potato chunks into the boiling water and cook until they can easily be pierced with a fork, about 20 minutes. Drain the sweet potatoes. Put the sweet potatoes in a bowl and mash with a wooden spoon, or pass them through a ricer into a bowl.

3. Add 3 tablespoons of the butter, the salt, and milk. Mix until smooth and well blended. Scrape the mashed sweet potatoes into a baking dish large enough to hold them. Spread in an even layer.

4. Put the brown sugar and pecans in a small bowl. In a small saucepan, melt the remaining 1 tablespoon butter. Drizzle over the nuts and sugar and stir to combine. Sprinkle the topping over the mashed sweet potatoes. Bake until the sweet potatoes are golden and the topping is crisp and melted, about 40 minutes. Serve immediately.

Sweet Potato Chips

Since sweet potatoes are oblong, they can easily be cut into uniform chips, perfect for baking. Serve the chips with homemade ketchup (see page 91) or a tangy yogurt dip (see page 19). [SERVES 4]

2 pounds sweet potatoes

3 tablespoons canola oil

2 tablespoons coarse sea salt

1. Preheat the oven to 375°F.

2. Using a sharp knife, cut the sweet potatoes crosswise into the thinnest possible slices. You can also use a mandoline to cut paper-thin slices.

3. Coat a baking sheet with 2 tablespoons of the canola oil. Place the sheet in the oven and heat for 5 to 7 minutes. The heated oil will help give the chips an crispy texture.

4. Put the sweet potato slices in a bowl. Drizzle with the remaining 1 tablespoon canola oil and toss gently to coat the slices. Remove the heated baking sheet from the oven and arrange the sweet potato slices in a single layer. Sprinkle with the salt. Bake, turning several times, until crisp, 25 to 30 minutes. Serve immediately.

KIDS CAN
rinse and dry the
sweet potatoes • coat the
baking sheet with oil •
toss the slices with oil •
arrange the slices on
the baking sheet

Spinach and Kale

Kale and spinach are called winter greens, a term that is somewhat of a misnomer since most varieties grow year-round. The name came about because these are the greens available in winter when the more delicate lettuces generally are not. Kids often find these nutrient-rich greens too strong in flavor, but the recipes here are designed to give the greens extra appeal. Spinach, which can sometimes taste metallic, is blended into a smoothie sweetened with apple and is used in a creamy filling for ravioli. Kale leaves are coated in seasonings and dried into chips for snacking.

Choosing: Select bunches of spinach with crisp, tender leaves. Bunches of kale should be sturdy and bright in color.

Storing: Remove and discard any damaged leaves from bunches of spinach and kale. Store in a plastic bag in the refrigerator for 5 to 7 days.

Varieties: kale: dinosaur, Lacinato, Russian; spinach: flat, savoy

Spinach and Ricotta Ravioli

Fresh spinach is a miracle green. Leafy and full when fresh, it reduces to one-fifth of its original volume when cooked. Chinese wonton wrappers stand in for pasta dough and kids will love stuffing them with filling. And after they eat them, they'll want to make them all the time. [SERVES 8]

1 bunch spinach, stems removed

1 cup ricotta cheese

2 eggs, 1 lightly beaten

3 tablespoons olive oil

½ teaspoon salt

¼ cup semolina flour or fine-ground cornmeal

32 square wonton wrappers

¼ cup grated pecorino or Parmesan cheese

1 tablespoon chopped flat-leaf parsley

KIDS CAN
rinse the spinach and remove stems • squeeze the cooked spinach • crack the eggs • grate the cheese • measure and mix the filling • help fill and fold the wrappers

1. Place a steamer rack in a large saucepan and add water to the pan. Put the spinach leaves in the pan, cover, and bring the water to a boil. Reduce the heat to medium and steam the spinach until wilted, about 5 minutes. Remove the spinach from the pan and let stand until it is cool enough to handle. Working over a bowl, squeeze out all the water from the spinach. Put the spinach on a cutting board and chop finely. Discard the water.

2. Place the chopped spinach in a large bowl. Add the ricotta, the whole egg, 1 tablespoon of the olive oil, and the salt. Mix until well blended.

3. Sprinkle about 1 tablespoon of the semolina flour on a work surface. Working in batches, lay out several wonton wrappers. Sprinkle the remaining semolina flour on a baking sheet. Place a generous teaspoonful of the spinach filling in the center of each wonton. Using a small brush or a finger, paint the edge of each wrapper with the beaten egg. Lift a corner of the wrapper and bring the wrapper over the filling to make a triangle. Press the edges together to seal. Set the finished ravioli on the semolina-covered baking sheet.

4. Bring a medium saucepan of water to a boil. Working in batches, slip the ravioli into the boiling water and cook for about 3 minutes, removing the ravioli from the pan as soon as they float to the surface. Place them in a serving bowl.

5. Add the remaining 2 tablespoons olive oil, the pecorino cheese, and the parsley to the ravioli. Toss gently to coat before serving.

Kale Chips

A fabulous alternative to potato chips, kale chips are both nutritious and delicious. The brewer's yeast, available at health-food stores, adds a little cheesy flavor. This recipe bakes up fast, so make sure that you check the kale regularly as it bakes because it can burn easily. [SERVES 6]

¼ cup olive oil

1 tablespoon lemon juice

1 tablespoon soy sauce

¼ cup brewer's yeast

1 bunch kale

KIDS CAN
measure the ingredients • rinse and dry the kale leaves • mix the leaves with the paste • place the leaves on the baking sheets

1. Preheat the oven to 425°F. Line two baking sheets with parchment paper.

2. Place the olive oil, lemon juice, soy sauce, and yeast in a bowl. Stir to form a smooth paste.

3. Place the whole kale leaves in the bowl. Use your hands to slather the kale pieces with the paste until they are fully coated.

4. Place the coated leaves on the baking sheets in a single layer so they are not overlapping. Bake the leaves, in batches, for 8 to 10 minutes until they are crisp. You will need to keep a close eye on the chips toward the end, as they tend to go from done to scorched quite suddenly.

5. Store the chips in airtight containers for up to 2 days.

Green Smoothie

If your kids are reluctant to eat their greens, maybe they will drink them!

[SERVES 1 TO 2]

1 cup trimmed spinach or
    kale leaves

½ cup freshly squeezed orange juice

¾ cup vanilla yogurt

½ apple, peeled, cored,
    and chopped

1 to 2 tablespoons maple syrup
    or honey

⅛ teaspoon cinnamon

Tear the leaves into pieces and place in a blender. Add the orange juice, yogurt, apple, maple syrup, and cinnamon. Purée until smooth. Pour into glasses to serve.

KIDS CAN
rinse and dry leaves and remove stems • tear the leaves • cut the apple into chunks • squeeze the orange juice, measure the yogurt • help blend the smoothie

Index

Table of Equivalents

The exact equivalents in the following tables have been rounded for convenience.

Liquid/Dry Measurements

U.S.	Metric
¼ teaspoon	1.25 milliliters
½ teaspoon	2.5 milliliters
1 teaspoon	5 milliliters
1 tablespoon (3 teaspoons)	15 milliliters
1 fluid ounce (2 tablespoons)	30 milliliters
¼ cup	60 milliliters
⅓ cup	80 milliliters
½ cup	120 milliliters
1 cup	240 milliliters
1 pint (2 cups)	480 milliliters
1 quart (4 cups, 32 ounces)	960 milliliters
1 gallon (4 quarts)	3.84 liters
1 ounce (by weight)	28 grams
1 pound	448 grams
2.2 pounds	1 kilogram

Lengths

U.S.	Metric
⅛ inch	3 millimeters
¼ inch	6 millimeters
½ inch	12 millimeters
1 inch	2.5 centimeters

Oven Temperature

Fahrenheit	Celsius	Gas
250	120	½
275	140	1
300	150	2
325	160	3
350	180	4
375	190	5
400	200	6
425	220	7
450	230	8
475	240	9
500	260	10